The Flippin' Awesome
BACKYARD GRIDDLE
COOKBOOK

The Flippin' Awesome

BACKYARD GRIDDLE

COOKBOOK

Tasty Recipes, Pro Tips and Bold Ideas
for Outdoor Flat-Top Grillin'

PAUL SIDORIAK

 ULYSSES PRESS

Published by
Ulysses Press
P.O. Box 3440
Berkeley, CA 94703
www.ulyssespress.com

ISBN: 978-1-61243-798-9
Library of Congress Catalog Number 2018930778

Printed in the United States by Versa Press
10 9 8 7 6

Acquisitions editor: Casie Vogel
Managing editor: Claire Chun
Editor: Lauren Harrison
Proofreader: Shayna Keyles
Front cover design: Malea Clark-Nicholson
Cover images: food © @DashofSavory except chicken yakitori © Paul Sidoriak; gray background © jirakit suparatanameta/shutterstock.com
Interior design/layout: what!design @ whatweb.com
Interior recipe images: © Paul Sidoriak; selected shots © @DashofSavory (see page 126 for a list of recipes)
Other images from shutterstock.com: gray background © jirakit suparatanameta; food press © Dani Simmonds; analog probe thermometer © Joy iStyleon; leave-in digital probe thermometer © byggarn.se; ginger/garlic © JIANG HONGYAN; lemons © AlenKadr

IMPORTANT NOTE TO READERS: This book is independently authored and published and no sponsorship or endorsement of this book by, and no affiliation with, any trademarked brands of the griddle grill or other trademarked brands or products mentioned within is claimed or suggested. All trademarks that appear in this book belong to their respective owners and are used here for informational purposes only. The author and publisher encourage readers to patronize the quality brands and products mentioned in this book. Take special note of the important safety warnings throughout this book, and always use customary precautions for safe food preparation, handling, and storage.

To Chery

Thank you for supporting my successes and failures, both on and off the grill.

Contents

Lunch 45

Dinner 71

Side Dishes 93

Snacks, Desserts, and Sauces 109

Introduction

The griddle grill has long been an indispensable fixture in diners and restaurants—the sizzling-hot top gives a great char to meat and anything you cook on it. But the old metal flat-top grills found in restaurants were big, heavy, and expensive, making them unappealing and impractical to the home cook, not to mention unsightly. Even the most gourmet home kitchens passed on a griddle grill in favor of other high-end domestic appliances.

Now, manufacturers make griddle grills that are more affordable, lighter, and more attractive. But what I most attribute to their significant spike in popularity is the adaptation of the fuel source: Today's griddle grills are designed to burn bottled propane.

They no longer require a connection to a fixed natural gas line that necessitates ventilation in a home kitchen. With bottled propane, the fuel source is portable, transforming the hulking, stationary grills into perfect outdoor cooking devices.

The first time I cooked on one of the recently manufactured outdoor griddle grills, it took me back more than 25 years to cooking as a high school kid in the snack bar and restaurant at the golf course where I worked. Nostalgic aromas wafted over me as I christened my griddle with its first pound of bacon, and I instantly remembered how fun it is to cook on the griddle grill. That night, we had smash-style bacon burgers on butter-crisped buns just like you get at the best old-fashioned burger joints. Because, guess what, you're using the same style of equipment the professionals are.

Cooking on a flat-top griddle grill is fun. This book will show you a bunch of the tips, techniques, and equipment the professionals use so you can easily re-create restaurant-quality experiences in your own backyard. I challenge you to think beyond pancakes, bacon, and hash browns, and consider cooking things like chicken Parmesan, scallops with asparagus tips, and crunchy ramen noodle and veggie stir-fries.

I will also talk about two-zone cooking, temperature control, and maintaining your flat-top griddle grill, and give you 50 fun and delicious recipes so you can be cooking like a pro in no time.

History of the Griddle Grill

Cooking on a griddle grill dates back to the Aztecs, who prepared corn tortillas and other foods on a flat surface made of clay, called the *comal*. The ancient griddle surfaces worked well for the some of the same reasons we still cook on them today: They maintain heat well, there's plenty of available cooking surface, and you simply place the surface over a fire or a bed of hot coals to operate. As time and technology advanced, Central Americans and Mexicans began constructing metal cooking surfaces called *planchas*, or metal plates.

And if you have ever been to a teppanyaki-style restaurant like Benihana, the griddle, or *teppan*, becomes a part of the experience and entertainment as you are seated at the griddle and have the opportunity to watch your food be cooked right in front of you.

Whether you are cooking on a plancha, comal, griddle, teppan, or hot plate, the principles are basically all the same. The cooking surface is sturdy, heavy, mostly flat, absorbs and retains heat well, and often develops a smoother, or seasoned, cooking surface the more frequently it is used. If you imagine what a native indigenous village would have been like at dinner time, there were most likely lots of mouths to feed. Griddle grills allow a lot of food to be prepared simultaneously so people could be fed at or around the same time.

Today, the griddle grill is an indispensable time-saving asset to any commercial kitchen. If you think about what a family of four may order at the local breakfast spot, cooking on the griddle grill is much faster than using individual pots and pans for each item. A short stack of pancakes, two eggs, bacon, home-fried potatoes, French toast, sausages, and a Denver omelet would take 11 pans and burners to make a breakfast for four. But with the griddle, it is one continually running cooking surface that takes far less time to clean between orders, making it much more popular than a pan and burner.

Why Cook on a Flat-Top Grill?

Flat-top griddle grills differ from regular grills because the griddle itself prevents the food from coming into direct contact with the flame. There are two significant benefits to this. One, the food can be juicier because it is not dried out by direct exposure to the heat source. The other benefit is that a griddle grill uses the principle of conduction, which transfers heat via the hot surface's direct contact with the food. Not only is this an efficient cooking method, but it promotes browning, also known as the Maillard reaction, which adds additional flavor and makes your food more visually appealing. One of the benefits of cooking on the griddle is that you increase the surface area on which the Maillard reaction can occur, essentially browning more of the meat.

Griddle Grills

There are a couple of griddle grill manufacturers that make the majority of backyard griddle grills seen on patios today. Both can be found in discount stores, box stores, sporting goods stores, hardware stores, and most places a gas grill can be purchased. As the popularity of the griddle grill continues to grow, there are bound to be other quality manufacturers in the marketplace.

Some griddle grills are small, lightweight, and very portable, making them perfect for a day at the beach or for an impromptu tailgate in the parking lot at a game or social event. Many of the smaller models use small, disposable propane canisters that are easy to find and not too bulky to pack around. Minor modifications allow you to replace the small canisters with large propane tanks if necessary. Other griddle grills will be more semi-permanent fixtures in your outdoor cooking space. Units will have three, four, six, or even more burners, which allows a larger cooking surface to be utilized and more food to be prepared at once. Typically, these larger multi-burner griddle grills will sit atop a built-in stand, with sturdy wheels and often side shelving for ingredients.

I am confident that as more people learn to enjoy cooking on the griddle grill, additional innovation will follow. I have seen smart outdoor islands built around griddle grills so guests can pull up a stool and watch the show as food is being prepared. One would guess that more precise temperature control, additional storage, integrated trash bins, refrigerators, grill covers, and even outdoor lighting and sound surrounding the griddle will soon follow, these things aren't available already.

Tools and Equipment

Spatulas. Spatulas are the most common griddle grilling accessory because they can move a good amount of food on the grill quickly and easily. I often wield one spatula in each hand so I can push food together and make more calculated flips.

You can find spatulas in all shapes and sizes, and chances are you have some already that will work well. Although normal kitchen spatulas can work just fine, they are often made of thin metal or plastic and are intended to flip food only weighing a few ounces. Griddle grill companies are coming out with sturdier models to help you flip your food. These have a stout, beefier construction so you can scrape under foods and flip heavier items without the tool bending or breaking. The griddle grill's cooking surface is tough, heavy, and made of metal, so it should easily be able to withstand a good scrape from a heavy-duty metal spatula. Save the plastic spatulas for your dedicated nonstick pan in the kitchen—in my experience, they break, melt, and warp much quicker than metal ones. A restaurant supply store is where the short-order cooks of America's best diners and greasy spoons get their spatulas, and it's a good option for you as well.

Squirt bottles. Squirt bottles are typically made of plastic, with a screw-top lid that tapers to a small opening. The bottles are supple, and liquids can be squeezed with a decent amount of accuracy onto or near your food or where you intend to cook. At the minimum, a squirt bottle with fresh water should be on hand at all times while using your griddle grill. A few drops of water on the griddle will instantly let you know just how hot or cold your cooking surface is. Many dishes benefit from the addition of water to the cooking surface, which will eventually evaporate and form steam. When the steam is captured under a cover, it is an effective way of transferring some heat to the top of your food, which is not touching the heated surface.

A bottle with cooking oil is also a must-have near your griddle grill. Using a squirt bottle is much easier, quicker, more precise, and less messy than pouring oil on the griddle directly from the bottle it came in.

Cooling racks. A simple wire cooling rack is very useful for the griddle grill. The close proximity of the rack to the griddle surface will keep food warm, but not allow it to continue to cook as much as if it were directly on the surface. A greasy meat like bacon will stay warm on the rack, dripping any extra rendered fat away and allowing you to directly cook your other foods and not worry about overcooking the bacon. A wire rack also works well if you are making something that cooks quickly and want your meal to all come together at the same time. For instance, if you were making bacon smash burgers, the bacon would take longer to cook than the burger patty. So you can cook the bacon in advance and set it aside to keep warm on the rack while you cook the burgers.

Broiler pans. Similar to cooling racks, broiler pans can work well to keep items warm. One advantage a broiling pan has over a cooling rack is that it has about a 1-inch-deep bottom that is normally used to catch drippings from food. This can be quite handy because you can add hot water to the bottom pan and it will keep food hot and ready when serving a crowd.

Covers and lids. Covers and lids are important for griddle grilling the same way they are important for cooking on your kitchen stove. Covering food intensifies the heat and allows food to cook more quickly. Covers are important for catching steam, and real time-savers when melting cheese onto something like a burger.

Butter wheel. Butter wheels are commonly found at a diner or where lots of food is getting made on the griddle. They are square, metal containers that hold one to two pounds of butter and sit directly on the surface of the flat-top griddle. Heat from the griddle melts the butter and keeps it melted. A wheel with perforations sits inside the container and protrudes over the top so that you can quickly roll a bun, slice of bread, basting brush, flat vegetable, or anything you wish to apply butter to directly.

Thrift Shopping

Thrift shopping can be a fun and inexpensive way to find all kinds of equipment you can use on the griddle grill at a fraction of the cost. I have many lids, pans, and flipping tools that are from the thrift store and basically dedicated to the griddle grill. They only come in the house for cleaning, and most of them cost less than a dollar. Think outside of the kitchen area at thrift stores too. Often, the hardware sections are a great spot to find deals on lightly used trowels, paint scrapers, and other tools that will work great on the griddle after a thorough cleaning. Keep your eyes out for kitchen towels as well when you're thrift shopping. Sometimes you can get a whole bag of them for about a dollar. They're great for wiping down your utensils and cook surface without your having to worry about grease or old food ruining them.

Food press. A bacon press or food press actually serves a few purposes on the griddle grill. Some bacon really likes to curl when you cook it, and weighing it down with a press for the most part prevents this from happening. It also helps render the fat quicker by pressing the food to the griddle. Bacon presses are simple. They're basically a round, square, or oval-shaped piece of metal that weighs your food down by pressing on it during cooking. Typically they have a handle that's engineered to keep cool so you can handle it easily, but the bacon press can get very hot, and some handles do a  better job than others at staying cool. I find the bacon press also works well to hold down sandwiches like the Cuban and can double as a device to make smash burgers. A brick can be covered in a few layers of heavy-duty foil and used as an inexpensive press.

Shop towels or rags. A clean griddle is a happy griddle, but grease and oil are common byproducts of the cooking process. To keep your griddle and work station clean, have on hand shop towels, rags, kitchen towels, and paper towels that do not leave behind fibers when you wipe down the cook surface and utensils. Hardware stores and big-box stores (or even thrift stores, see page 13) often sell these types of towels for a fraction of the cost you would pay at a kitchen or bath store, and by having dedicated towels for your griddle grill, you are less likely to be tempted to get yourself in trouble by using the nice ones.

Trowels and scrapers. Anyone who has smoothed over concrete, fixed a hole in Sheetrock, or scraped paint from a wall has used very sturdy metal tools to get the job done. Scrapers, trowels, and putty knives all make wonderful tools on the griddle grill for flattening a burger, scraping off old food, moving around liquids and oils, and even flipping the occasional pancake. If you decide to use a nontraditional tool, consider one that is brand-new, and make sure to clean and sanitize with hot soapy water, then dry well.

Thermometers. Thermometers are an important part of any type of cooking. There are a few basic types I recommend for cooking on the griddle grill.

Instant-read thermometers are made to be inserted in the food briefly to check the temperature of what you are cooking. Digital ones are great because they take the food's temperature quickly. They come in all price ranges and you can get a good, very accurate model for around $30. Analog probe thermometers (or chef thermometers, as I like to call them) do not require batteries and are about the size of a pencil, with an analog readout dial on the top that shows your food's temperature. A good one is usually around $10 and comes with a sheath and a clip to

Analog probe thermometer

secure it in your pocket just like a pen. These take the temperature slower than a digital thermometer, but they work well.

An *infrared thermometer* shoots a laser at the cook surface or wherever you point it and almost instantly displays the surface temperature. Infrared thermometers are fantastic when you have a newer griddle grill and are learning the nuances of how quickly the cook surface heats or which parts of your griddle may be prone to having hot or cool spots during the cook. Infrared thermometers are also fun to use. After I take the temperature of my cooking surface, I often find myself taking the temperature of many things irrelevant to cooking, like my patio furniture, the tomato plants, or the tops of my feet. For about $25, an infrared thermometer is a very useful device.

The *leave-in digital probe thermometer* is a digital probe tethered to a digital display that tells you the temperature of what you are cooking. These are ideal for cooking large cuts of meat like thick pork chops because you can monitor the internal temperature without guessing. Prices of these thermometers vary based on additional features and how accurate they are. You do get what you pay for, but if you choose one with good reviews, you can find one that will last a long time for about $60.

Leave-in digital probe thermometer

Maintenance

Maintaining your griddle grill is very important so that the next time you get the urge to cook, it is ready to go at a moment's notice. Preparing the surface for your next cook is relatively easy to do as you finish your cook. As I shut down my grill, I use these steps to prepare for next time:

1. With a firm scraper or spatula, consolidate all extra oils, fats, and bits of food that may have collected, then discard.

2. Use a towel to wipe the griddle surface clean and leave only an extremely thin film of oil. Remove any pooling, drops, drips, or streaks.

3. If your most recent cook involved any sugary foods like maple bacon or a sweet sauce, be sure to scrape the sugary residue from the griddle surface. Often a combination of water and a little elbow grease on a hot griddle will get the residue to release quickly.

4. After the griddle grill has cooled, be sure to cover it and protect it from the elements. A couple tablespoons of oil should be applied to the surface of the griddle grill before you cover your griddle for storage.

5. If you are not planning on using the griddle grill in the immediate future, consider disconnecting the fuel source just to be safe.

Seasoning the Grill

Seasoning your grill is important because it allows the cooking surface to develop a hardened, often nonstick coating that will allow foods to release much more easily from the griddle. Some griddles require seasoning prior to cooking, and others come pre-seasoned from the factory. I recommend following your manufacturer's suggestions on how to properly season and care for your griddle surface. Here are a few tips I have found helpful when seasoning or re-seasoning a griddle surface:

Before you ignite your griddle grill for the first time, give it a quick wipe down with soap and water, even if it looks clean. Be sure to rinse well.

Ignite your griddle grill and add about a cup of water to the surface as it comes up to temperature. As the water begins to boil and evaporate, wad up a clean towel and use tongs or a spatula to carefully wipe the griddle surface of any debris or oils.

When all the water and steam has evaporated and burned off the cooking surface, turn the griddle grill off and allow it to sit for about 10 minutes.

After the griddle has cooled some—at least enough so you don't burn your hands—but is still warm, pour 1 to 2 tablespoons of oil on the griddle and wipe it all over the surface with a handful of paper towels, taking care to get the corners, sides, and even the back of the cooking surface.

Re-ignite your griddle grill to high heat and allow the thin coating of oil to smoke and burn off until the smoking stops. Typically, this can take up to 20 minutes.

When the smoke has stopped, turn off the grill and allow it to cool for about 5 minutes before wiping any pooling or streaks clean with a paper towel.

It has been my experience that the griddle will season in patterns that line up to the shape of the burners underneath them. A first attempt often leaves a nice, seasoned patina in an oval or circular pattern on the center of your griddle. I will repeat this seasoning process four to six times to make sure that the entire griddle grill is seasoned, but your griddle may only need to be seasoned two or three times. I have found that it works best if you only use the smallest amount of oil required to coat the surface and allow it to burn until the smoke has completely stopped between seasoning attempts. If your griddle is mostly seasoned but some small portions are not quite as complete as the others, not to worry. Just go ahead and cook on it. The lighter areas will darken after a few cooks.

Note: There are many oils and fats that work for seasoning the griddle grill. Flaxseed oil is one that I've used on many occasions for seasoning both the griddle grill and cast-iron skillets. It can usually be found in the refrigerated section of health food stores or in the natural foods department at larger supermarkets. If you cannot find flaxseed oil, vegetable oil, peanut oil, lard, bacon grease, or tallow will all work just as well.

Preparing to Cook

One thing you will probably notice in this book is that I preheat my griddle grill to either medium, medium-high, or high heat before almost every recipe. The more you cook on the griddle grill, the sooner you will learn about how long it takes for your grill to reach its desired pre-cook temperature. If a griddle is too cool when you begin cooking, some foods will take much longer to start browning and the food will absorb more oil than you desire, making the dish soggy and greasy. On the other hand, if the griddle is blazing hot, delicate foods like a burger bun may burn on the bottom without being warmed all the way to the top. The infrared thermometer will give you an accurate temperature reading, and every grill is different, so use my suggestions as a guide and then dial in the temperatures as you get more experienced.

Always Be Prepared!

Mise en place is a French term for having everything in place before you begin cooking. Mise en place is especially important for griddle grilling because the cooking can often happen quickly and you do not want to be fumbling around looking for utensils like a spatula, or making multiple trips back to the kitchen for things like butter or water.

When preparing your mise en place, consider the entire cook. What ingredients will you be using? Which tools will you need? Did you remember cooking oils, seasonings, and a plate or platter to present or share your food when it's ready? Having a garbage can nearby is also an important part of mise en place so you can quickly dispose of any scraps you may have .

Two-Zone Cooking

If you have more than one zone on your griddle grill, you can use two-zone cooking, meaning you'll have a hotter area and a cooler area on the cooking surface that work to your benefit. This method works better with larger griddle grills than smaller ones because the heat is more spread out. One of my griddle grills has four burners, each with a different temperature controller. Most commonly, I will preheat the griddle grill with the right three burners on and the fourth left burner completely off. When the right portion of the griddle gets to my desired temperature, I turn off the second from the left burner too. This leaves me with the

Utilizing two-zone cooking

right side of the griddle at about my desired cooking temperature, and the griddle gets cooler the farther you go to the left of the cooking surface, creating two temperature zones.

The benefit of two-zone cooking is that with some planning, you can start to cook foods that take longer earlier than foods that take only a moment to cook. For example, if I want to make bacon and eggs, bacon takes 8 to 10 minutes to cook, while eggs take only 2 to 3 minutes. I start cooking the bacon in the hot zone, and when it is about done, I transfer it to the cooler zone where it stays warm while I quickly cook the eggs. This also works especially well when you're cooking for a crowd who aren't all eating at the same time. Burgers, potatoes, pancakes, veggies, and other foods can be held warm on the cooler zone until you are ready to serve.

Your Very First Cook

Hopefully by now you have had a chance to set up the griddle grill in an area safe for outdoor cooking and have had a chance to season the surface to your liking. The question I see time and time again is, what should I cook first? The first thing I like to cook on the griddle is always bacon, which serves a couple of purposes. Bacon is a visual thing to cook, so you don't need to worry as much about cooking it to a safe internal temperature. If bacon looks cooked and is relatively crunchy, chances are that you and your guests are going to enjoy it. Bacon also releases a good amount of grease, which will additionally coat the griddle and assist

with the seasoning process. You can practice moving the grease from one area on the griddle to another. You can also pool your grease in a certain area or just practice corralling the grease into the grease tray, if you grill has one, and then dispose of it later.

Although you could just simply eat bacon for your first meal, most folks need a little more variety. I would suggest something simple, something you enjoy, and something that fits nicely between two slices of bread or a bun. Burgers would be a natural first thing to make on the griddle. Chances are you have had burgers with varying degrees of quality over the years. This burger could be the best one you have ever had, and I would almost guarantee it won't be the worst. If you decide to go a different route and cook whole cuts of meat like chicken breast, pork chops, or steak, I suggest making sure your meat is very evenly flattened out, boneless, and not much thicker than about a half an inch thick.

Before you start cooking the main event, ask yourself: Is the grill hot? Is it well oiled? Has the oil come up to temperature? Do I have all the ingredients for this cook ready to go, do I have a cold beverage to enjoy while I am cooking, and do I have a clean plate or platter to serve or transfer the food to when I'm done cooking?

Three of the most important ingredients in outdoor cooking are self-confidence, deep breaths, and a big smile. If you incorporate those into your cooking, the results will almost always be better than you had planned.

Breakfast

BUTTERMILK PANCAKES

Buttermilk pancakes are a staple at many diners and breakfast restaurants. They are fluffy and delicious, and the hint of sour from the buttermilk balances wonderfully with sweet pancake syrup and butter.

Makes 8 pancakes, serves 2 to 4

2 cups all-purpose flour

3 tablespoons sugar

2 teaspoons baking powder

2 teaspoons baking soda

pinch kosher salt

2 eggs

2½ cups buttermilk

¼ cup melted butter

1. Sift the flour, sugar, baking powder, baking soda, and salt together in a large bowl.

2. In a medium bowl, whisk the eggs, buttermilk, and melted butter together until frothy, then pour into the dry ingredients. Mix until well combined but do not overmix. Small lumps will be fine. Let sit at room temperature for 20 to 30 minutes while your grill heats up.

3. Bring the griddle grill to medium-high heat. Oil the griddle and allow it to heat until the oil is shimmering but not smoking.

4. Pour about ¼ cup batter onto the griddle grill for each pancake. The pancakes should slowly begin to form bubbles. After 2 to 4 minutes, when the bubbles pop and leave small holes, flip the pancake. Cook for an additional 2 minutes.

CHORIZO BREAKFAST TACOS

These breakfast tacos are savory and creamy. Corn tortillas are gluten-free and make a perfect holder for the eggs and chorizo, but feel free to use flour tortillas if you prefer.

Serves 3

4 eggs

¼ cup milk

½ pound chorizo

butter, as needed

½ cup chopped green pepper

½ cup diced sweet onion

6 corn tortillas

½ cup shredded cheddar cheese

cooking oil, as needed

1. Crack the eggs into a medium bowl and whisk with the milk until well mixed.

2. Bring the griddle grill to medium-high heat.

3. When the grill is hot, begin to cook the chorizo. As the chorizo cooks, chop it continually with a stiff spatula or metal scraper to promote even cooking and browning while it breaks into small pieces. Cover the chorizo and allow it to cook completely.

4. While the chorizo continues to cook, melt a couple of pats of butter on the griddle and sauté the pepper and onion until the peppers begin to wilt and the onions start to become translucent. Combine the chorizo and vegetables and spread them out evenly on the cooking surface.

5. If needed, add more butter to make sure the griddle is well greased before you pour the egg mixture into the chopped chorizo and veggies. Using a wide spatula or scraper, stir the egg mixture while it cooks and the eggs form curds. As the eggs solidify, scrape the eggs, chorizo and veggies aside and cover to keep warm.

6. Spread a thin coat of oil on the griddle and allow it to heat until shimmering. Place the tortillas in the oil and cook for about 2 minutes per side.

7. Uncover the chorizo mixture and add the cheese on top. Cook until the cheese melts.

8. Assemble the tacos by dividing the chorizo mixture into thirds and scooping it into a double-layered tortilla, then top with cheese.

POTATO PANCAKES

Enjoyable at any time of the day, the potato pancake is a crispy treat that's quick and easy to cook on the griddle. They can be served sweet or savory and are delicious when topped with fresh herbs and a dollop of sour cream.

Makes about 8, serves 2 to 4

2 eggs

¼ cup milk

1½ cups russet potato, peeled and shredded

¼ cup all-purpose flour

¼ cup finely diced onion

¼ cup finely chopped green onion

1 teaspoon baking powder

1 teaspoon salt

1 teaspoon pepper

cooking oil, as needed

1. In a large bowl, beat the eggs and milk until frothy. Add the remaining ingredients and stir to combine. The batter should be moist throughout but not pooling with liquid. Allow to rest for 20 minutes while the grill heats up.

2. Bring the griddle grill to medium-high heat.

3. Add a thin coat of oil to the cooking surface, and when it begins to shimmer, add about ¼ cup of potato pancake batter to the griddle for each pancake. Press the batter to flatten and cook each side for 3 to 4 minutes until golden brown.

ICE CREAM FRENCH TOAST

I prefer to use Texas toast for this recipe, but day-old French bread, sourdough bread, or even a hard roll can work well, and you can cut it to your desired thickness. If possible, allow your bread to sit out for a couple hours or overnight to expose it to air and firm it up a bit. Other variations I love for this recipe are to substitute almond liqueur for the vanilla extract or replace the cinnamon with ground nutmeg.

Serves 4

1 cup melted vanilla ice cream

3 eggs

1 teaspoon vanilla extract

pinch of ground cinnamon

8 slices Texas toast or other thick-cut bread

cooking oil, as needed

1. Combine the melted ice cream, eggs, vanilla extract, and cinnamon in a bowl wide enough for the bread to be easily dipped into. Mix very well or until frothy.

2. Bring the griddle grill to medium-high heat and coat the surface with oil. When the oil begins to shimmer, dip each side of the bread into the egg batter so it lightly coats each side. Allow any additional batter to drain back into the bowl.

3. Place the bread on the griddle. Cook for 3 to 4 minutes per side, or until the French toast is golden brown. Repeat with the remaining ingredients.

PIGS IN A BLANKET

A local pancake parlor serves pigs in a blanket. I enjoy them so much, I am barely even certain that they serve other items. When the pancake wrapped around sausage mixes with some syrup and butter, something delicious happens. This is a great way to start your morning.

Serves 4

Buttermilk Pancake batter (page 23)

8 breakfast sausage links

1. Make the buttermilk pancake batter.

2. Bring the griddle grill to medium-high heat.

3. Cook the breakfast sausage links until they are completely cooked through, with the juices running clear, or when they reach an internal temperature of 165°F, then set aside and keep warm.

4. Follow the directions for making buttermilk pancakes. Using your spatula, coax the pancake to roll around the sausage link like a blanket. Allow to continue cooking with the sausage in the middle until the pancake is fully cooked.

EGGS BELLEDICT

When it comes to brunch, eggs Benedict are the belle of the ball. Here, we make eggs Benedict more portable, using a fried egg instead of poached and containing it inside of a sweet ring of bell pepper. Using Jarlsberg cheese instead of the traditional Hollandaise sauce makes this dish much simpler and less messy than a traditional eggs Benedict.

Serves 2

1 medium red or green bell pepper

2 English muffins

2 eggs

4 slices Canadian bacon

½ cup very finely shredded Jarlsberg cheese

butter, as needed

1. Bring the griddle grill to medium heat. Cut the uneven bottom off the bell pepper, then cut two rings of pepper about ½ inch thick.

2. Coat the griddle with a good amount of butter. Separate the English muffins and place the uncut-sides on the griddle to begin warming. Place the bell pepper rings on the griddle and cook for 2 minutes. Flip the peppers, then flip the English muffins to heat the other sides.

3. Crack an egg and carefully drop it into one of the bell pepper rings. Scoot the other pepper ring close by and repeat with the second egg. Using a cover that's just bigger than the peppers, cover the eggs and allow them to cook for 1 minute.

4. While the eggs are cooking, warm the Canadian bacon on the grilling surface.

5. Remove the cover from the eggs and squirt water around the grilling surface very close to the eggs, and immediately cover the eggs again to capture the steam and assist with cooking the whites and yolks. Cook for another minute, then cover each of the eggs with half of the cheese. The finer the cheese is grated, the more quickly it will melt, so I use a very fine grater or even a Microplane. Squirt the perimeter of the eggs again and cover to catch the steam, allowing the cheese to melt.

6. Remove the English muffins from the griddle and put 2 slices of Canadian bacon on top of each. Uncover the eggs, and using a spatula, remove the pepper ring containing the egg and slide it onto the Canadian bacon. Top with the other half of the English muffin.

DINER-STYLE OMELET

Omelets are versatile—you can make them simply with a few eggs, or freestyle and take advantage of a variety of ingredients to make them even more delicious. When I make omelets for friends and family, I often use whatever is on hand in the fridge to elevate the dish and make it special. This recipe uses just a few ingredients, but you can really break out of your shell and go wild with fillers and toppings. Breakfast joints and diners will often use a commercial mixer to create a very frothy and aerated egg mixture, which most think results in a much fluffier omelet. Using a fork or a whisk to beat the eggs is fine, but try and capture as much air into the mixture as you can while you are beating them. If you have an immersion blender, electric hand mixer, or stand mixer with a whisk attachment, these are all great tools to get the eggs to that frothy, restaurant consistency.

Serves 1

½ cup diced red bell pepper

½ cup sliced mushrooms

½ teaspoon garlic salt

2 eggs plus 2 egg yolks

½ cup shredded cheddar-Jack cheese blend, or 2 slices cheese

butter, as needed

salt and pepper, to taste

cilantro, to serve (optional)

1. Bring the griddle grill to medium-low heat.

2. Butter a portion of your griddle grill and begin to slowly sauté the peppers and mushrooms. After about 3 minutes, give the veggies a stir and sprinkle on the garlic salt, then cover.

3. Beat the eggs in a medium bowl until quite frothy. With a large spatula, move the pepper and mushroom mixture to the side of the griddle. Melt plenty of butter over a large area on the griddle and very slowly pour the eggs onto the cooking surface. The eggs will run a bit, and if you are able to use the side of the spatula to shape them into a circle or square, they will be easier to flip later on.

4. Allow the eggs to cook slowly without much poking or prodding. After about 3 minutes, you will see the eggs start to bubble as they cook. Some portions of the omelet will be firm, and some portions will be runny and raw. Distribute the peppers and mushrooms evenly across the omelet the same way you would top a pizza, in a thin layer. When about 80 percent of the egg has solidified, add the cheese in an even layer.

5. At this point, your omelet should have very little runny or visibly raw egg remaining. With a long spatula, scrape under the omelet with a quick wrist motion to make sure the egg is released from the griddle before you attempt to finish. To fold the omelet in half, slide the spatula under the omelet until the entire width of the spatula is covered, and with a lift and twist, lift the spatula and twist your wrist so the omelet folds over and flops onto itself.

6. Cook for about another minute and serve with salt and pepper to taste. Garnish with cilantro, if desired.

JOHNNY CAKES

The first time I had Johnny Cakes was at a diner in Rhode Island. The addition of cornmeal to the batter makes the cakes richer and more decadent than normal pancakes. Delicious with butter and syrup, but even better when enjoyed with fresh strawberries.

Makes 8 pancakes, serves 2 to 4

2 eggs

1⅓ cups milk

1 tablespoon honey

¼ cup cooking oil

1½ cups all-purpose flour

½ cup fine cornmeal

4 teaspoons baking powder

1 tablespoon sugar

1 teaspoon salt

1. Whisk the eggs, milk, honey, and oil in a medium bowl until frothy. Combine the flour, cornmeal, baking powder, sugar, and salt in a large bowl and stir to combine.

2. Add the wet ingredients to the dry ingredients and stir until well-incorporated and free of clumps. Let sit for 20 minutes while your grill heats up.

3. Bring the griddle grill to medium-high heat. Oil the griddle and allow it to heat until the oil is shimmering but not smoking.

4. Pour about ¼ cup of batter onto the griddle grill for each pancake. The pancakes should slowly begin to form bubbles. After 2 to 4 minutes, when the bubbles pop and leave small holes, flip the pancakes. Cook for an additional 2 minutes.

CREPES

Crepes are easy to make, and once you get going, they come off the griddle grill quite fast, allowing you to make a pile of them in a short amount of time. You can't go wrong with a plain crepe topped with a pat of butter and powdered sugar or your favorite syrup. But the reason I really love making these breakfast favorites is that they are a blank canvas for filling with ingredients from sweet to savory; they can also be served for any meal of the day. Crepes can be made ahead and frozen.

Makes about 8 crepes

1 cup all-purpose flour

1½ cups milk

½ cup water

2 eggs

1 teaspoon grated lemon zest

2 pinches salt

2 tablespoons melted butter, plus more as needed for the griddle

1. Place all the ingredients except the butter in a blender and blend for 30 to 45 seconds until a smooth batter forms. If necessary, scrape down the sides of the blender so all the ingredients are incorporated, and blend again. Allow the batter to rest for 30 minutes.

2. Bring the griddle grill to medium heat. Butter about a 10-inch square on the griddle grill, then pour ¼ cup of the batter in the center.

3. Spread the crepe batter into a circle with the measuring cup or use a crepe spreader to create a thin, round layer on the griddle. Cook for about 90 seconds or until most of the batter has set. Flip and cook for another 60 to 90 seconds until it is between yellow and golden brown in color. (You can cook the crepes to your desired doneness, but I find cooking them to a yellowish color leaning toward golden brown is best for rolling and stuffing.)

STEAK AND MUSHROOM WITH BALSAMIC SAUCE

This variation is enjoyable hot or cold.

Serves 2

2 tablespoons butter

8 cremini mushrooms, sliced

1 tablespoon minced garlic

1 teaspoon salt, plus more to taste

1 teaspoon pepper, plus more to taste

Balsamic Griddle Sauce (page 122), as needed

6-ounce beef tenderloin fillet, cut in half lengthwise

2 prepared crepes

cooking oil, as needed

1. Over medium heat, melt the butter and sauté the mushrooms with the garlic and 1 teaspoon each of salt and pepper.

2. The salt will help release the moisture from the mushrooms. When this begins, add ¾ cup of the Balsamic Griddle Sauce to the mushrooms and cover. Stir occasionally for 6 to 8 minutes, and set aside to keep warm.

3. Increase the heat on the griddle grill to medium high and while it is heating, scrape and clean any residual balsamic sauce from the cooking surface so it does not burn.

4. Pat the beef dry with paper towels, and season liberally with salt and pepper.

5. Add cooking oil to the griddle, and when it begins to shimmer, add the steak and sear for 3 minutes. Flip and sear for an additional 1 to 3 minutes, based on your desired doneness.

6. Allow the steak to rest for 10 minutes, then cut across the grain into thin slices. Arrange the steak on a crepe and top with mushrooms.

STRAWBERRY, BANANA, AND HAZELNUT-CHOCOLATE

This sweet version is one of the simplest to make, but it is among the most memorable of all the crepes I have had since I tried one in Paris many years ago. It makes a delicious breakfast, a light dessert, or a satisfying snack anytime your sweet tooth speaks to you.

Serves 2

6 tablespoons hazelnut-chocolate spread

2 prepared crepes

8 large strawberries, sliced

1 banana, sliced

powdered sugar

1. Spread half the hazelnut-chocolate spread on each of the crepes and divide the fruit evenly as a topping.

2. Fold the crepes over the filling and garnish with powdered sugar.

HAM AND SWISS

Serves 2

2 tablespoons oil

½ red bell pepper, thinly sliced

6 thin slices Black Forest ham

4 thin slices Swiss cheese

2 prepared crepes

2 teaspoons Dijon mustard

1. Bring the griddle grill to medium and heat the oil. Sauté the bell pepper strips for 5 to 7 minutes, until wilted. Set aside and keep warm.

2. Spread ham slices out on the griddle grill and warm them for about 5 minutes on one side. Flip the ham and arrange into two piles of three slices, letting the slices overlap.

3. Place two slices of cheese on each of the piles of ham, add a few tablespoons of water to the griddle, and cover to help the cheese melt.

4. While the cheese is melting, warm the crepes on the griddle and spread half the mustard on each. Top with the ham and melted cheese and sauteed bell peppers. Fold and serve.

CHICKEN BACON ARTICHOKE

Serves 2

4 slices bacon

8 ounces chicken breast, cut into small cubes

White Wine Griddle Sauce (page 123)

3 marinated artichoke hearts, quartered

2 prepared crepes

⅓ cup ranch dressing

salt and pepper, to taste

1. Bring the griddle grill to medium-high heat and cook the bacon. Remove and keep warm.

2. In the bacon fat, sauté the cubed chicken with salt and pepper for 4 minutes, with very little movement, allowing the chicken to brown. Add the White Wine Griddle Sauce as needed and cover to finish cooking an additional 4 to 6 minutes, or until the chicken is done. Remove and keep warm.

3. Sauté the marinated artichokes in the residual bits of cooked chicken on the griddle grill for 3 to 5 minutes until warm and slightly brown.

4. Spread about half of the ranch dressing on each crepe. Fill the crepes with chicken, bacon, and artichoke pieces.

CRAB AND AVOCADO

Serves 2

1 tablespoon oil

1 shallot, minced

1 clove garlic, minced

pinch of salt

pinch of pepper

1 cup cooked jumbo lump crab meat

2 prepared crepes

spritz Lemon Griddle Sauce (page 122) or White Wine Griddle Sauce (page 123)

1 avocado, pitted, peeled, and thinly sliced

1. Over medium heat, warm the oil and sauté the shallots and garlic until the shallot is translucent. Add the salt, pepper, and the crab to the shallots, along with a spritz of griddle sauce, and cook for 3 to 5 minutes, covered, stirring occasionally until the crab is warmed.

2. Fill each crepe with the crab meat mixture and fan sliced avocado over the top.

Lunch

SMASHED BURGERS

Smashed burgers are one of my favorite things to make on the griddle grill. Using freshly ground chuck with a good amount of fat and minimal seasoning allows the natural beef flavors to shine. Smashing the burger onto the griddle surface increases the surface area to promote browning in the beef and helps develop a deliciously flavorful crust. To achieve the perfect smashed burger, you'll need parchment paper, a bacon press, and a heavy-duty spatula.

Serves 4

4 burger buns

1 pound ground chuck (80/20), divided into 4-ounce balls

4 slices American cheese

salt and pepper, to taste

1. Bring the griddle grill to high heat. Cut 4 squares of parchment paper. Butter the grill surface and toast the insides of the burger buns for 1 to 2 minutes until a golden brown crust forms and the bun has warmed. Set aside.

2. Scrape your griddle surface clean with a scraper or spatula. Place the ground beef balls on the griddle surface, spacing them 6 to 8 inches apart. Place a parchment paper square down on one of the ground beef balls, and smash it to about ¼ inch thick with a bacon press. Remove parchment paper, and repeat with the remaining beef balls. Season the raw sides of the burgers liberally with salt and pepper.

3. Allow the smashed beef to cook for about 2 minutes without disturbing. Hold a heavy-duty spatula and scrape under the burger to release it from the griddle and take all of the browned bits with it. Flip the burger, and quickly repeat with the others.

4. Cover the burgers with cheese slices and allow to cook for an additional 2 minutes, or until the cheese begins to melt. If you desire the cheese to be extra melty, cover the burgers after the cheese is added.

5. Using your heavy-duty spatula, scrape each burger again at an aggressive angle to release from the griddle and slide them onto your browned burger buns.

6. You can dress these burgers up with lettuce, tomato, onion, and a variety of condiments or sauces, but I prefer to just enjoy the rich, meaty flavor of the burger, and the smooth mouthfeel of the buttery toasted bun.

Burgers

Few foods spark as much nostalgia as the burger. Burgers are quick, convenient, and typically inexpensive. But what they lack in cost, they make up for in flavor, and they're all a little bit different. Sure the meat, seasonings, toppings, and buns have something to do with how the burgers taste, but the way the meat is cooked, and what it is cooked on, makes all the difference. Some diners, burger shacks, and roadside stands have been cooking on the same flat-top grill daily for decades, and it leaves an unmistakably delicious flavor on the food, which you can replicate at home with your griddle grill.

RANCH-STYLE TURKEY BURGERS WITH MOZZARELLA

I always wonder why turkey burgers aren't more popular. Turkey meat has a bit more flavor than chicken or other white meats, and takes on seasonings and flavors quite well. When choosing turkey for turkey burgers, if there is a lean variety, choose something different. If you grind your own turkey, adding pork fat or even bacon will add even more flavor to the mix. The mozzarella will melt and become crisp on the bottom of the burger, but deliciously melty and stringy on the inside. The combination of the creamy melted mozzarella with the turkey and ranch seasonings is a match made in heaven. Bacon and avocado slices are a delicious topping for this burger.

Serves 4

1 pound ground turkey

1 egg

¼ cup powdered ranch seasoning

¼ cup mozzarella crumbles

¼ cup seasoned bread crumbs

4 burger buns

butter, as needed

cooking oil, as needed

1. Mix the turkey, egg, ranch seasoning, mozzarella crumbles, and bread crumbs together in a mixing bowl until well combined. Divide the mixture into four patties and set aside.

2. Bring the griddle grill to medium-high heat. Add enough butter to coat the grilling surface and cook the burger buns in the butter for 2 to 3 minutes or until golden brown and warmed. Set aside.

3. Coat the griddle with a thin layer of cooking oil. Cook the burgers, covered, for 4 to 6 minutes per side or until the internal temperature of the turkey reaches at least 165°F. Serve on warmed burger buns.

BEHEMOTH BACON BURGERS

When I close my eyes and think about the perfect bacon burger, this classic comes to mind. Every bite has a variety of flavors and textures that march to the same beat. Personally, a ⅓-pound burger is the perfect size for me, but I have seen this burger in ½-, ¾-, and even 1-pound sizes at specialty burger restaurants.

Serves 2

2 large sesame-seed burger buns

6 strips bacon

1 tablespoon salt

1 tablespoon pepper

1 tablespoon onion powder

1 tablespoon garlic powder

2 (⅓-pound) burger patties

4 slices cheese (optional)

butter, as needed

TOPPINGS

mayonnaise

mustard

ketchup

lettuce

1 medium, firm tomato, cut into thick slices

1 medium, sweet onion, cut into rings

dill pickle chips

1. Bring the griddle grill to medium-high heat. Add some butter to coat the grilling surface and cook the sesame seeded buns in the butter for 2 to 3 minutes, or until golden brown and warmed. Set aside.

2. Place the bacon on the griddle. Cook for 6 to 8 minutes, or until your desired doneness. Set aside the bacon and keep warm.

3. Combine the salt, pepper, onion powder, and garlic powder in a small bowl. Season both sides of the burger patties with the seasoning mix. Place the patties on the griddle grill where the bacon had cooked and cover. Cook for 4 to 5 minutes, or until the tops of the burgers begin to sweat red juices. Flip, add cheese if using, and cover, cooking for another 2 to 3 minutes or until they reach your desired doneness. I often cook to 135°F and check the temperature with an instant-read thermometer.

4. To build the burger, spread mayo on the bottom bun. Add the burger with melted cheese and bacon plus the toppings of your choice. Cover with the top bun and enjoy.

#CHOPPEDCHEESE

I schemed up this burger recipe last summer because I was in the mood for something between a patty melt and a grilled cheese. I had never seen or heard of a burger like this, but after one bite I knew it was fun to cook and a delicious recipe worth repeating. When I posted it on Instagram, someone told me it's called a #ChoppedCheese and is quite popular at bodegas in the Bronx and other areas of New York City. It turns out the sandwich has quite a cult following, and this is my version. For the bread, rolls including grinder, hoagie, hard, sandwich, wedge, po' boy, sub, or similar will work just fine, depending on what's available where you live.

Serves 3

1 pound ground beef

1 small onion, minced

1 tablespoon onion powder

1 tablespoon garlic powder

1 tablespoon pepper

1 teaspoon salt

9 slices American cheese

3 hero rolls, or other similar bread

butter or cooking oil, as needed

TOPPINGS

lettuce

tomato

ketchup

mayonnaise

pickles

mushrooms

bell peppers

jalapenos

marinara sauce

Thousand Island dressing

breaded mozzarella sticks

1. Bring the griddle grill to medium heat. Coat the surface with butter or your preferred cooking oil. Place the meat on one side of the griddle. Place the onion on a different part of the griddle and allow the onions to sauté until they become translucent.

2. While the meat cooks, chop it into small pieces with a spatula or scraper. Season with the onion powder, garlic powder, pepper, and salt, and continue to chop and cook the meat until it turns from red to pink, and then brown.

3. When the pieces are small and barely cooked through, add the onions to the meat and divide into three equal portions and cover each portion with three slices of cheese spread evenly across the meat. Cover to allow the cheese to melt quicker.

4. Scoop up one of the meat portions and serve it on the bread. Adding any combination of some of the suggested toppings would make this sandwich even more delicious.

TURKEY AND MELTED BRIE SANDWICH WITH GREEN CHILES

Sometimes you're just after a melty, creamy, gooey sandwich with lots of pizzazz. This sandwich is extremely creamy from the melted Brie, but the green chiles add a peppery zing to every bite and elevate the flavor of the turkey slices. A thick toasted bread like sourdough works well to hold together all the melty cheese and juices.

Serves 1

3 tablespoons roasted, diced green chiles

6 ounces sliced deli turkey

2 slices thick-sliced bread

4 ounces Brie, thinly sliced

butter, as needed

1. Bring the griddle grill to medium heat.

2. Melt butter on the griddle and sauté the green chiles for about 3 minutes, to warm them and add a little caramelization.

3. Add more butter to the grilling surface and fan out the turkey slices on the griddle to warm them and get a slightly browned color. Cook for 2 to 3 minutes per side.

4. Butter the griddle again and place the two slices of bread on the griddle. Lay half of the sliced Brie on each of the slices of bread to allow the Brie to warm. Place half of the warmed turkey slices on top of the Brie on each slice of bread and allow the warm turkey to assist in melting the cheese. Add the warmed chiles to one slice of bread and use the other slice to cover the chiles, making a sandwich.

5. Cover and allow the sandwich to continue to cook for about 4 minutes, flipping once, until the cheese is fully melted. The sandwich will be very hot and gooey with the melted cheese, so consider allowing it to rest for about 4 minutes before eating—if you can resist.

CHICKEN FAJITA SANDWICH ON A QUESADILLA BUN

I worked in one of those restaurants known for fajitas many years ago, and have always been captivated by how many people order them. But I get it: The flavors work together, they arrive on a sizzling skillet, and you get to assemble them yourself at the table. This chicken fajita sandwich combines the sizzling flavors of the fajita with the crunchy, cheesy goodness of a quesadilla—possibly the best of both worlds.

Serves 2

FOR THE FAJITA CHICKEN MARINADE:

½ cup cooking oil

1 ounce tequila

2 tablespoons Worcestershire sauce

1 tablespoon hot sauce

4 cloves garlic, minced

juice of 1 lemon

juice of 1 lime

1 tablespoon ground cumin

1 tablespoon garlic powder

1 tablespoon onion powder

1 teaspoon salt

1 teaspoon pepper

FOR THE FAJITAS:

1 (8-ounce) chicken breast, sliced into strips

½ Lemon Griddle Sauce (page 122), plus more for cooking

8 medium-sized flour tortillas

2 cups shredded cheddar-Jack cheese blend

½ green bell pepper, cut into strips

½ red bell pepper, cut into strips

1 medium, sweet onion cut into strips

¾ cup prepared salsa, divided

salt and pepper, to taste

1. Mix all the fajita marinade ingredients together in a large bowl. Add the sliced chicken to the mixture, cover, and allow to marinate in refrigerator for 4 to 6 hours or overnight.

2. Bring the griddle grill to medium-high heat. Place the chicken on the grill. Discard any leftover marinade. Cook the chicken strips, covered, for 10 to 12 minutes until cooked through, turning occasionally and adding Lemon Griddle Sauce from time to time to promote steaming.

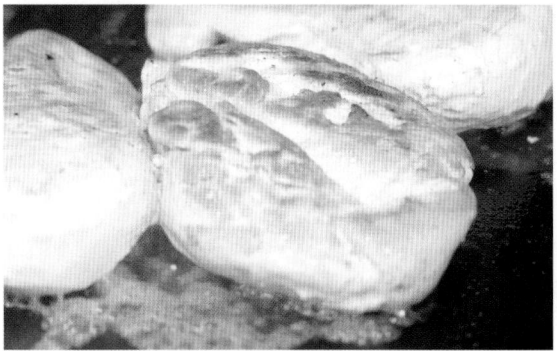

3. While the chicken is cooking, place four of the tortillas on the griddle and allow them to warm. As the tortillas begin to warm, divide the cheese between them and cover each with a second tortilla to make the quesadilla buns. Flip the quesadillas after 3 minutes and allow the other sides to warm and the cheese to melt for another 3 minutes. Set aside and keep warm.

4. Warm a little oil on the grill, add the peppers and onions, and allow to sauté for 3 to 5 minutes until wilted. As peppers and onions begin to wilt, sprinkle with salt and pepper, add about ½ cup Lemon Griddle Sauce, and cook for about 3 more minutes, until the onions are translucent.

5. When the chicken is fully cooked, assemble by placing a quesadilla on a plate and covering with salsa. Add chicken, peppers and onions, and top with an additional quesadilla.

DINER-STYLE PATTY MELT

I love the diner-style patty melt because it feels like I am getting a few meals in one. The grilled onions and mushrooms melt together with Swiss cheese and wrap the burger in a warm blanket of flavors. The bread becomes crispy and crunchy, soaking up the many different flavors in its path.

Serves 2

2 cups sliced mushrooms

1 cup sliced sweet onions

2 (¼-pound) ground beef burger patties

butter, as needed

4 slices deli rye or dark rye bread

4 slices Swiss cheese

cooking oil, as needed

salt and pepper, to taste

1. Bring the griddle grill to medium-high heat.

2. Put a thin layer of oil on the cooking surface and spread the onions and mushrooms on the griddle, keeping them separate. Sprinkle salt and pepper on the mushrooms and onion slices. Allow the mushrooms to sauté for 6 to 8 minutes, stirring and flipping frequently. The salt should pull moisture from the mushrooms and they should shrink significantly in size, taking on a lightly browned color. The onions should cook until translucent with light caramelization, about 5 minutes. Allow the cooked mushrooms and onions to stay warm on a cooler side of the griddle grill.

3. Season the burgers with salt and pepper on both sides. Cook on the griddle for 4 to 6 minutes on each side, or until they reach your desired temperature. Set aside to keep warm.

4. To assemble, butter the griddle well and place all four slices of bread in the butter. Cover each slice of bread with a slice of Swiss cheese. Then, divide the onion and mushroom mixture onto two slices of bread. Place a cooked burger patty on each bread slice with the onion and mushroom mixture. Top each with a slice of bread. At this point, the bread should have browned some, and the cheese should have started melting. I prefer bread that is crisper and cheese that is fully melted, so I will flip my assembled patty melt and allow it to continue to cook. Covering the patty melt for the final few minutes will also help the cheese melt more quickly.

CHEESESTEAK HOAGIE

The cheesesteak has to be one of the undisputed kings of the griddle-grilling experience. Anyone who has had a real-deal Philadelphia cheesesteak sandwich can tell you there is something about it that is pure perfection. You can get the taste of Philly at home anytime you're in the mood, but they're so quick and easy to make, you may as well invite a few friends over to join you. Although this version of cheesesteak does not include mushrooms, feel free to add them, or freestyle with additional ingredients like jalapenos, marinara sauce, or even bacon, if the mood strikes you.

Shaved ribeye steak can often be found in the freezer section of major grocery stores and works well for this recipe, direct from the freezer. A good butcher will often slice a ribeye super thinly for you if you ask nicely and give some advance notice. If not, a ribeye roast can be cut thinly if you let it sit in the freezer for close to an hour and then carefully cut it with a very sharp knife.

Serves 2

2 French bread sandwich buns

1 medium bell pepper, thinly sliced

1 medium onion, thinly sliced

2 cloves garlic, finely minced

12 ounces very thinly sliced ribeye roast

8 slices American cheese

cooking oil, as needed

butter, as needed

salt and pepper, to taste

1. Bring the griddle grill to medium-high heat. Melt butter on the griddle and toast the cut sides of the sandwich buns until they turn a light golden brown. Set aside on a serving platter.

2. Oil the griddle grill and turn the heat up to high. Begin to sauté the peppers, onions, and garlic.

3. Spread the ribeye roast out on the griddle grill, and as liquid begins to release from the meat, season with salt and pepper, and use two heavy-duty spatulas to chop the meat into shreds.

4. As the sautéed peppers and onions become wilted and translucent, after about 4 minutes, the shredded meat should be turning from raw to almost cooked. Mix the meat with the peppers and onions and continue to cook until the meat is just cooked through.

5. Divide the meat into two loose piles that will fit under a grill lid. Add 4 slices of the cheese to each pile of meat. Add a squirt of water around the meat and cover. Allow to cook for 2 to 3 minutes, until the cheese is melted and gooey.

 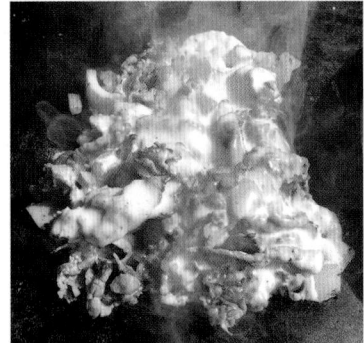

6. Using both spatulas, scoop up the cheesesteak filling and scrape it onto the buns. Serve with plenty of napkins.

GROUND PORK BANH MI

This Vietnamese sandwich has so many fun things happening at the same time, and every bite is like unwrapping a small gift of flavor from a pile of presents.

Makes 4 sandwiches

¼ cup rice wine vinegar

3 tablespoons sugar

1 cup carrot matchsticks

¼ cup mayonnaise

½ cup minced cilantro, divided

1 tablespoon sriracha

1 pound ground pork shoulder

¼ cup grated onion

1 clove garlic, minced

3 tablespoons soy sauce

2 tablespoons fish sauce

1 teaspoon salt, divided

1 teaspoon pepper

4 French bread–style sandwich buns

cilantro sprigs, for garnish

1. In a microwave, warm the rice wine vinegar with the sugar and ½ teaspoon salt until dissolved, about 45 seconds. Pour the warm vinegar mixture over the carrot matchsticks in a medium bowl and refrigerate to cool. In a small bowl, mix the mayonnaise with 1 tablespoon of the cilantro and the sriracha. Set aside and keep refrigerated.

2. In a large bowl, mix the ground pork with remaining minced cilantro, onion, garlic, soy sauce, fish sauce, the remaining salt, and pepper. Allow the mixture to rest and develop flavors covered for 1 hour to overnight in the refrigerator.

3. Bring the griddle grill to medium-high heat. With a spatula, chop and saute the pork for 5 minutes, then cover and cook an additional 4 to 6 minutes, adding water to the grill to promote steaming.

4. Cut the sandwich buns in half and allow them to warm on the griddle grill until they are heated and take on a small amount of color. Divide and spread the cilantro mayonnaise on one side of each bun. Place ¼ of the pork on each bun and garnish with pickled carrots and cilantro sprigs.

CUBAN SANDWICH

The first time I made Cuban sandwiches at a party, our team was playing Miami in a late season game. What is so great about these sandwiches is that you can prepare them in advance and cook them to order when your gang gets hungry. The sweet and salty flavors mingle with the acidity of the pickles and are rounded out with the creaminess of Swiss cheese. I add mayonnaise to the sandwich for an extra pop of flavor. To press these sandwiches, you'll want to have foil and a bacon press or cast-iron skillet on hand.

Serves 2

2 Italian sandwich rolls

¼ cup mayonnaise

¼ cup yellow mustard

8 slices honey ham

8 slices roast deli pork

8 slices Swiss cheese

6 pickle chips

butter, as needed

1. Bring the griddle grill to medium heat.

2. While the griddle is heating, build your sandwiches. Cut the sandwich rolls lengthwise without cutting all the way through and place them on a cutting board with the cut side facing up.

3. Slather one side of each roll with mayonnaise and mustard.

4. Place 2 slices of Swiss cheese on one side of each roll. Layer 4 slices of ham and 4 slices of pork on top of the cheese, and cover the meat with half of the pickles. Cover the pickles with the remaining slices of cheese.

5. Close the sandwich and prepare the griddle with a generous amount of butter. Place a bacon press or cast-iron skillet on the grill surface to heat up for about 5 minutes before cooking.

6. Place the sandwiches on the melted butter and cover the sandwiches with foil. Weigh the sandwiches down with the hot bacon press or cast-iron skillet. Allow the sandwiches to cook for 5 to 7 minutes.

7. Flip the sandwich and return the weight to the other side. Cook for an additional 3 minutes, or until the cheese is very well melted and all of the ingredients are hot throughout.

TRIPLE-DECKER MONTE CRISTO SANDWICH

The Monte Cristo is the perfect balance of breakfast and lunch. Grilling the ham and turkey slices ahead of time packs more flavor into the sandwich.

Serves 1 or 2

3 ounces Black Forest deli ham

3 ounces smoked deli turkey

3 slices thick-sliced bread or Texas toast

2 slices Swiss cheese

2 slices American cheese

2 tablespoons mayonnaise, divided

1 cup Buttermilk Pancake batter (page 23) plus 2 tablespoons water

powdered sugar, for dusting

¼ cup warm maple syrup, to serve

¼ cup raspberry jam, to serve

cooking oil, as needed

butter, as needed

1. Bring the griddle grill to medium-high heat.

2. Melt a little butter on the grill and cook the ham and turkey slices for 3 to 4 minutes, or until the meat is slightly caramelized and takes on some color.

3. Remove the crusts from the bread. Add half the mayonnaise to a slice of bread, then add the Swiss cheese, and then the ham. Cover with a second slice of bread. Add the turkey slices, then the American cheese. Coat the third slice of bread with the remaining mayonnaise and put it face-down on the top of the sandwich.

4. Place a large piece of plastic wrap on a flat surface. Put the sandwich in the middle of the plastic wrap. Fold the plastic wrap over the sandwich and press down firmly on it to compress and push some air out of the bread. Wrap the sandwich tightly by rolling it forward to the edge of the plastic wrap and tuck the ends over the top to secure. Allow the sandwich to rest in the refrigerator for 2 to 6 hours.

5. Bring the griddle to medium heat. Oil the griddle well.

6. Lightly dredge the sandwich in the pancake batter and place on the griddle. Cook each side for 3 to 5 minutes, covered. When each of the sides has lightly browned, use tongs and cook the edges of the sandwich for 45 to 60 seconds per edge. The pancake batter should form a nice crust, but you should also see evidence of the cheese melting inside the sandwich.

7. Traditionally, the Monte Cristo sandwich is cut into triangles and served with a dusting of powdered sugar. Having warm maple syrup and raspberry jam on hand for dipping only sweetens the deal.

NOT-YOUR-ORDINARY REUBEN

There is probably no right or wrong way to enjoy a Reuben sandwich, but the adaptations I make here are minor. I use pastrami instead of corned beef because I love the additional flavor the pepper brings. I also use Thousand Island instead of Russian dressing because I love the pickled relish taste on this sandwich.

Serves 1

4 slices deli pastrami

1 tablespoon Dijon mustard

3 tablespoons Thousand Island dressing

2 slices rye bread

4 slices Swiss cheese

2 tablespoons mayonnaise

1. Bring the griddle grill to medium heat.

2. Cook the sliced pastrami on the grill for 3 to 5 minutes, turning frequently, until it begins to brown and shrink. Smother the slices with Dijon mustard and set aside.

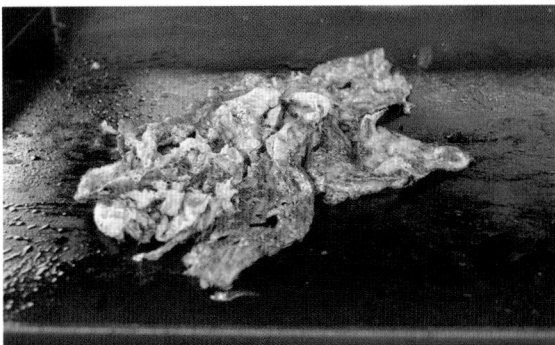

3. Assemble the sandwich by spreading the Thousand Island dressing on each slice of bread. Then top each bread slice with two pieces of Swiss cheese, allowing ¾ inch to hang out over the edge of the crust. Add the meat to the sandwich and slather with mayonnaise, then close the sandwich.

4. Grill the sandwich, covered, over medium heat for 3 to 4 minutes on each side. Allow the Swiss cheese to melt onto the griddle surface and become crispy. Take care when flipping or removing the sandwich from the griddle to scrape underneath the cheese and protect its shape.

Dinner

CHICKEN YAKITORI

Chicken yakitori is a wonderfully flavorful preparation of chicken thighs commonly found at Japanese restaurants or Asian food trucks. Some things just work, and the marriage of ginger, garlic, soy sauce, and a few other ingredients does not disappoint. This dish is perfect as a main course, but it will also make a fantastic appetizer at your next party, and if you manage to have leftovers, it is delicious cold the next day.

Serves 8

½ cup water

¼ cup cornstarch

2 pounds boneless, skinless chicken thighs, cut into 1-inch cubes

2 cloves garlic, minced

2 tablespoons soy sauce or tamari sauce

1 tablespoon black pepper

2 tablespoons freshly grated ginger

1 tablespoon sesame oil

cooking oil, as needed

sesame seeds, for garnish

finely chopped green onion, for garnish

SAUCE:

½ cup soy sauce or tamari sauce

½ cup low-sodium chicken broth

2 tablespoons rice wine vinegar

2 tablespoons mirin

½ cup brown sugar

2 tablespoons honey

2 tablespoons freshly grated ginger

3 cloves garlic, minced

1. Whisk together the water and cornstarch in a medium bowl to create a slurry. Make sure all the cornstarch has mixed with the water and there are no lumps. Divide in half.

2. Marinate the chicken in one half of the cornstarch slurry, along with the garlic, soy sauce or tamari sauce, black pepper, ginger, and sesame oil. Leave covered in the refrigerator, for 30 minutes or up to 4 hours.

3. While the chicken is marinating, combine the sauce ingredients in a saucepan and heat over medium-high on a stovetop. Bring to a slow boil, stirring frequently to dissolve the sugar. Slowly boil for about 3 minutes and remove from the heat. Stir in the remaining half of the cornstarch slurry. Return to medium heat and continue stirring until the sauce comes back to a slow boil. The cornstarch should rapidly thicken the mixture. Allow the sauce to simmer, stirring frequently, for another 90 seconds, or until the sauce thickens enough to coat the back of a spoon. Divide the sauce in half and set aside.

4. Bring the griddle grill to medium-high heat. Skewer the chicken cubes close together on metal skewers. Discard any leftover marinade.

5. Oil the grill well and cook the chicken for 8 to 12 minutes, covered, turning a quarter turn every couple of minutes to promote even browning. If the chicken is browning quicker than it is cooking, or sooner than you had hoped for, squirt some water onto the grilling surface and skewers and allow the steam to assist in the cooking process.

6. Brush half of the sauce on the chicken and allow it to reduce further on the skewer. Pay careful attention to the griddle temperature so the marinade does not burn. Paint each side of the chicken in layers to create a saucy coating on the skewers. Remove the chicken when it reaches a safe internal temperature of 165°F.

7. Garnish with sesame seeds and green onions. Serve with the remaining sauce for dipping.

CHICKEN PARMESAN WITH GRILLED TOMATO SAUCE

One of the benefits of cooking outside, especially in the summer months, is that you don't heat up the kitchen on a warm day. When I got a taste for chicken Parmesan on a hot August day, the griddle grill did not disappoint, and I have not made this dish in the house again since.

Serves 2

2 eggs

¼ cup water

2 cups all-purpose flour

1 tablespoon salt

1 tablespoon pepper

1 tablespoon garlic powder

1 tablespoon onion powder

1 tablespoon dried oregano

2 cups panko bread crumbs

2 boneless, skinless chicken breasts, tenderloins removed

very thinly sliced basil, for garnish

½ cup shredded mozzarella cheese, to serve

cooking oil or butter, as needed

MARINARA SAUCE

2 cups diced canned tomatoes	1 teaspoon salt
1 tablespoon tomato paste	1 teaspoon dried basil
1 teaspoon minced garlic	1 teaspoon dried oregano
water, as needed	pinch of sugar
1 teaspoon garlic powder	cooking oil, as needed

1. In a large, shallow bowl, beat the eggs with the water until well mixed. In a separate large, shallow dish, stir together the flour, salt, pepper, garlic powder, onion powder, and oregano. Put the bread crumbs in a third dish.

2. Pound the chicken breasts flat—½ inch thick is ideal. Pat the chicken very dry with paper towels. Arrange your breading dishes in an assembly line with flour/herbs mix, then egg wash, then the bread crumbs. Dip one piece of chicken in the seasoned flour, flipping multiple times to coat. You want the chicken to be well coated, but in a thin layer with no clumping. Then dredge the chicken in the egg wash on both sides, so it is evenly covered in a thin layer of egg glue. Dip the floured and egged chicken in the bread crumbs and flip two or three times. The breading will make a shell around the chicken, so it is important that it is evenly coated. If you have a bald spot, dip the area missing breading back in the egg wash, and then back into the bread crumbs. Repeat with other chicken breast. Place on a dry plate in the refrigerator, uncovered, for 30 minutes.

3. To make the marinara sauce, bring the griddle grill to medium heat, about 325°F. Lightly coat the surface with cooking oil or butter. Sauté the diced tomato and garlic together for 5 to 7 minutes, allowing the tomatoes to break down and wilt slightly, with minimal browning. Transfer the cooked tomato mixture to a blender and add the remaining sauce ingredients. Blend at low speed for about a minute and then gradually increase the speed until the sauce is extremely smooth. If it is too thick, add water 1 tablespoon at a time until it reaches your desired consistency.

4. Clean the griddle well after sautéing the tomatoes. Reheat to about 375°F. Coat the grill with a moderate amount of oil. When the oil begins to shimmer and before it spreads too far, place the breaded chicken breasts down on the griddle. It is important to lock on the breading and allow it to adhere to the chicken, so allow it to cook for 2 to 3 minutes before moving it. Add more oil to the griddle, close to the chicken. When the oil starts to shimmer, flip the uncooked side of the chicken onto the hot oil and cover. Cook for 3 to 5 minutes, covered and undisturbed, and then remove the lid and flip again, adding more oil if necessary. At this point, the breading should be well-bonded to the chicken. Cook to a safe internal temperature of 165°F.

5. To finish, flip the chicken one last time and coat each piece with ½ cup of the marinara, or enough to cover the chicken to your liking. Top the chicken and marinara with mozzarella. Getting the cheese to melt happens by adding a small amount of water to the griddle grill like a halo around the chicken and immediately covering it, capturing the steam. If a little water touches the side of the chicken, it will not ruin the dish, but take care not to saturate the chicken's breaded crust in water, which can make it soggy. Serve with ribbons of sliced basil.

VEGGIE STIR-FRY

Stir-fry is so much fun to make on the griddle grill and can be modified with many different ingredients. This veggie stir-fry is fantastic for a Meatless Monday meal. It is hearty, satisfying, and great to serve if you have vegetarians in the mix. I use fresh and canned vegetables here, but there are many freshly frozen options you can use that are quite convenient.

Serves 2 or 3

3 cups shredded green cabbage

1 cup shredded red cabbage

1 cup diced celery

1 cup diced carrot

1 cup diced onion

1 cup sliced mushrooms

1 (8-ounce) can sliced water chestnuts, drained

1 (8-ounce) can baby corn, drained

3 tablespoons minced ginger

3 tablespoons minced garlic

1 cup Asian Griddle Sauce (page 121)

vegetable or peanut oil, as needed

salt, to taste

1. Bring the griddle grill to medium heat.

2. Coat the griddle with your favorite light oil, like vegetable or peanut, and heat until shimmering. Spread all the ingredients, except the salt and griddle sauce, on the griddle in an even layer.

3. Sprinkle a small amount of salt, up to 1 teaspoon, over the vegetables and allow to cook undisturbed for about 3 minutes. The salt will release liquids from the vegetables as they begin to cook.

4. Using one or two large spatulas, flip all the vegetables and allow them to cook for another 3 to 4 minutes. The vegetables will begin to wilt as they cook and you can corral them toward the middle of the griddle. Stir in the Asian Griddle Sauce and cover to finish cooking, 2 to 3 minutes more.

SHRIMP WITH CHEESY POLENTA CAKES

Some food combinations just work well together. We do not have to understand why to appreciate how delicious the flavors are. Recently, one of my favorites has been shrimp and grits. In this recipe, we make the grits ahead of time and finish them on the griddle grill as polenta cakes. It's one of those dishes that works well as a main course, but can also be a fantastic appetizer or lunch when served with a salad.

Serves 4 to 6

3 cups water

1 tablespoon garlic salt

1 cup fine cornmeal/polenta

2 cups shredded white cheddar cheese, divided

¼ cup (½ stick) cold butter, divided

1 pound jumbo 21/25 shrimp, peeled and deveined

White Wine Griddle Sauce (page 123), as needed

cooking oil, as needed

1. Make the polenta cake in advance by bringing water and garlic salt to a boil in a medium pot over high heat. Reduce the heat to low, and add the polenta, stirring frequently to prevent clumping. Using a long-handled wooden spoon or heat-resistant spatula, stir constantly as you allow the polenta to cook at a very slow boil over low heat. Boiling polenta is extremely hot and unpleasant if it hits your skin, so take care to prevent it from splashing on you while cooking. Cook for 12 to 15 minutes, until it has thickened to a coarse pudding-like consistency, then stir in half the cheese and butter. Stirring frequently, allow the butter and cheese to melt completely, then add the remaining butter and cheese. Stir until fully melted. Carefully pour the polenta into a square baking pan or muffin tins, in a layer about an inch thick. Allow to cool 4 to 6 hours or overnight, covered in the refrigerator.

2. Bring the griddle grill to medium-high heat. Remove the polenta from the refrigerator and invert it onto a flat surface to take it out of the pan. If you used a baking pan, cut the polenta into squares based on how many servings you intend to make.

3. Grease the griddle grill well with cooking oil, and once it begins to shimmer, add the shrimp on one side and the polenta cakes on the other. Cover the shrimp and allow both the shrimp and the cakes to cook undisturbed for 3 to 4 minutes.

4. Flip all the shrimp and deglaze with some of the White Wine Griddle Sauce, then cover. To flip the polenta cakes, use a sturdy spatula, and scrape under the cake, making sure all the golden brown crust remains intact. The shrimp should be done when pink throughout and curled from head to tail, after about 6 minutes.

5. Serve the shrimp on top of the polenta cakes.

RAMEN PORK AND VEGGIE CAKE

Okonomiyaki cakes are a popular Japanese-style pancake. This is my version of the Hiroshima okonomiyaki, which includes ramen noodles and omits the traditional pancake batter. I understand okonomiyaki means "grilled as you like it," or something close to that, which is one of the reasons I love this dish. I use ground pork, but you can use other meats and vegetables to make the dish more interesting. The transformation of the ramen noodle from soft and supple to crispy and crunchy is what keeps me making this delicious dish over and over again.

Serves 2

¼ pound ground pork

¼ cup soy sauce

2 tablespoons minced ginger

2 tablespoons minced garlic

2 tablespoons sesame oil

2 (6-ounce) packages cooked ramen noodles

2 cups chopped cabbage

¾ cup chopped kale

⅓ cup shredded carrot

Asian Griddle Sauce (page 121), as needed

cooking oil, as needed

1. Bring the griddle grill to medium-high heat. Place the ground pork on the griddle and using a spatula, or spatula and scraper, cook the pork, chopping it into fine pieces to promote even cooking and texture.

2. After about 4 minutes, add the soy sauce, ginger, garlic, and sesame oil to the pork. Continue to cook for another 1 to 2 minutes until the liquids have reduced, and slide to a cooler area on the griddle.

3. Add oil to your cooking surface and allow it to heat until shimmering. Spread the cooked ramen noodles in a thin layer across the griddle, taking advantage of the surface area it provides. The noodles are hydrated with water, and we want the water to evaporate some, eventually making the noodles crispy. In the process, the noodles will go from wet to gooey and gummy, and then begin turning brown and crispy. It is important to allow the noodles to cook, but not burn on the griddle. When you first flip the noodles, after about 5 minutes, work in batches and make sure to scrape as many of the noodle bits from the grilling surface as you can. Add more oil as needed to prevent sticking and promote browning, but use it sparingly.

4. Add the cabbage, kale, carrot, and pork onto half of the noodles. Layer the other noodles on top of the mixture and allow the noodles to help wilt the veggies. Spread all the ingredients out across the griddle and flip the noodles and veggies from the outside inward to help the veggies make more contact with the griddle, and add some Asian Griddle Sauce for additional flavor.

5. As the griddle sauce reduces, and eventually evaporates, you will notice the noodles and veggies start to brown and get quite crispy. This is what you are after. The outer layer of the noodle cake should be crispy and crunchy, and the inner noodles should still be a bit supple, balancing the textures.

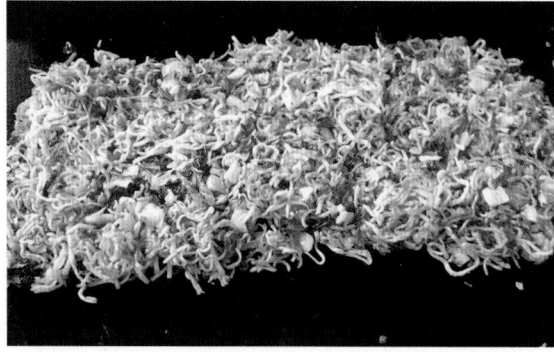

EASY CHICKPEA FALAFEL

Falafel is a staple of Mediterranean cuisine and can easily be served as a main dish over a salad of freshly tossed greens, or as a bite-size snack or appetizer whenever the mood strikes you. The fun thing about this dish is that you can make the falafel patties ahead of time and freeze them for when you are ready to heat them up on the griddle grill.

Serves 4

1 (16-ounce) can chickpeas, drained

¾ cup diced sweet onion

¼ cup diced shallot

2 tablespoons freshly chopped parsley

4 cloves garlic, minced

1 teaspoon ground cumin

1 teaspoon paprika

1 teaspoon olive oil

1 teaspoon salt

1 teaspoon pepper

¼ cup all-purpose flour

1 teaspoon baking powder

cooking oil, as needed

1. Combine all the ingredients except the flour and baking powder in a food processor or blender. Blend until smooth with some small chunks remaining, scraping the sides of the bowl 2 to 3 times to make sure all of the ingredients are incorporated.

2. Transfer the falafel mix to a medium bowl. Sift and then stir in the flour and baking powder. Mix by hand until the mixture absorbs the flour and becomes firmer. Cover tightly and allow to rest in the refrigerator for at least an hour.

3. Bring the griddle grill to medium heat and form the falafel into 4 patties just under 1 inch thick.

4. Add a generous amount of oil to your cooking surface and allow it to heat until shimmering. Place the patties in the hot oil and allow to cook 3 to 4 minutes, covered. Flip and cook, covered, for an additional 3 to 4 minutes, until heated through and a golden crust has formed.

ROULADE OF BEEF WITH BUTTERED NOODLES

When we were growing up, my German grandmother, Hildegard, made this dish for her seven kids and many grandchildren in large cast-iron skillets. The flavors are very unique but well balanced, and the reduced braising liquid begs to be drizzled over noodles and even mopped up with fresh bread. Something magical happens and you taste each of the ingredients with every bite.

Serves 4

6 strips bacon

1 cup diced onion

1 pound thin cut sirloin tip or eye of round beef (about 8 slices)

½ cup yellow mustard

8 long thin dill pickle slices, cut into ribbons

16 ounces American-style lager

16 ounces beef stock

4 cups noodles, cooked and cooled

½ cup finely chopped fresh parsley, for garnish

cooking oil, as needed

salt and pepper, to taste

1. Bring the griddle to medium-high heat. Cook the bacon for about 10 minutes until crisp. Cool, crumble into small bits, and set aside.

2. Sauté the diced onion in the bacon grease for about 5 minutes, until the onions are translucent. Any browned bits of bacon that you can get to release from the griddle and onto the onions will reward you with additional flavor. Allow the onions to cool.

3. To assemble the roulade, sprinkle both sides of a slice of beef with salt and pepper and lay it on a cutting board. If necessary, square off the sides and ends to make a rectangle. Slather a thin coat of mustard on the beef. Place about 2 tablespoons each of the crumbled bacon and onion along one long edge of the beef slice, taking care to leave a perimeter of ¾ inch free of toppings. Add ribbons of pickles to the top of the onion and bacon mixture.

4. Starting at the covered edge of the beef slice, tightly roll the beef, bacon, onions, and pickles toward the opposite side, into a cigar shape. Take care to keep the roulade tight to keep the ingredients inside. Repeat with remaining beef slices and ingredients.

5. To cook, bring the griddle grill to about medium-high heat. Add cooking oil to the grill and when it shimmers, place the roulades directly on the griddle with the seam sides down. You want the seam of the roulade to seal as it sears to keep the ingredients from falling out. Allow the seam side to cook for 3 minutes, then roll the roulades to brown the rest of the meat for another 2 to 3 minutes per side or until you get a consistently browned exterior.

6. To braise the roulades, place a skillet directly on the griddle surface. Put all of the roulades inside of the skillet in a single layer. In a large bowl, mix the lager and broth and use 1 to 2 cups as braising liquid, or enough so the meat is about 80 percent covered in liquid. (If you prefer to omit the beer, you can simply double the amount of beef broth.)

7. Cover the skillet and leave a small gap so the steam can escape. Allow the liquid to reduce by about half, 15 to 20 minutes, then carefully rotate the roulades so the portion that was not in the braising liquid is now covered. Add an additional 1 to 2 cups of liquid and allow it to reduce over medium heat for 15 to 20 minutes. The meat should be fork tender with just the right amount of give from your initial searing efforts.

8. While the liquid is reducing, coat a clean part of your griddle with butter and cook the noodles in the butter. Flip with a large spatula to get some brownness and texture on them.

9. To serve, place a bed of noodles on each plate with two roulades on top. Any reduced braising liquid can be whimsically drizzled on top of the noodles and beef for an additional boost of flavor. Garnish with chopped parsley.

ASIAN-SEARED SALMON

Salmon is readily available year round and relatively easy to source at your local grocery store. Most of us are not lucky enough to catch our own salmon, so purveyors are flash-freezing salmon within hours of being caught, often in individual portions that defrost quickly. I often take salmon from the freezer midafternoon and have it on the dinner table a few hours later. Salmon is a favorite because it is low in calories, is a fantastic source of omega-3 fatty acids, and can be served over a salad, with grains, or on a bed of stir-fried vegetables.

Serves 2

2 (4-ounce) salmon fillets

¾ cup Asian Griddle Sauce (page 121), plus more as needed

cooking oil, as needed

salt and pepper, to taste

1. Wash the salmon fillets and pat dry. Check for pin bones by placing salmon skin-side down on a cutting board and gently running your fingers across the thicker parts of the fillet. If you feel any bones, use a pair of tweezers to remove them before cooking.

2. Flip the salmon over, skin-side up. Typically, the salmon will resemble the shape of an airplane wing: thick, oval-round on one end, and tapering off to a very thin side on the other end. Make three or four ¼-inch cuts across the skin on the thickest part of the filet. This will allow the filet to cook a bit more evenly and with less curling when it is on the griddle. Season both sides of the filet with salt and pepper and make sure to get some seasoning into the areas where you scored the skin.

3. Bring the griddle grill to medium-high heat and add cooking oil to the surface. When the oil is shimmering, place the salmon skin-side down and cook for 3 or 4 minutes without disturbing. This develops a crispy crust on the salmon skin that many people find quite delicious.

4. When you are ready to flip, place the spatula on the griddle grill at an aggressive 15-degree angle and scrape under the skin to release and flip the salmon.

5. Shake the Asian Griddle Sauce well and add about ¾ cup to the griddle near the salmon. Slide the salmon into the sauce, cover it, and allow it to steam cook for another 5 minutes. If desired, flip the salmon an additional time and allow it to bathe in the Asian Griddle Sauce before plating.

SCALLOPS AND ASPARAGUS TIPS

Scallops are one of the most perfect bounties of the sea for the home cook. They are full of flavor, simple to prep and cook, and easy on the wallet. Scallops are often available in varieties of wet or dry. A wet scallop means it has been soaked in a preserving phosphate solution, and a dry scallop has not. If you have the option, go with the dry one. However, if a wet scallop is the only thing available, you can soak the scallop in cold water for about a half-hour to remove a good majority of the preservative.

There are only two basic prep techniques for scallops. The scallop has a small muscle called the abductor muscle. It is a thin strip about the width of a pencil eraser which can easily be peeled off and discarded. If you miss removing the abductor muscle, do not worry, it is edible. The other important step to get scallops ready for the griddle is to make sure they are patted dry with a few layers of paper towels. Typically, I place them out on a few layers of paper towels and let them sit on one side for about 4 minutes, and then flip and repeat.

This recipe comes together very quickly, so be prepared and have your ingredients ready to go.

Serves 2

2 cups asparagus tips

8 large dry scallops

White Wine Griddle Sauce (page 123), as needed

butter, as needed

cooking oil, as needed

salt and pepper, to taste

1. Bring the griddle grill to medium-high heat.

2. Coat the griddle with cooking oil, and when it begins to shimmer, place the asparagus on the grill. Allow to cook for 2 minutes, stirring frequently.

3. Cover the asparagus and place the scallops on the griddle with plenty of room between them. Scallops will only cook for 2 minutes per side, so set a timer.

4. Just before you flip the scallops, give the asparagus a squirt of the White Wine Griddle Sauce and add a pat of butter. Flip the scallops and allow them to cook for another 2 minutes until done. Season with salt and pepper to taste.

5. Serve the asparagus alongside the scallops.

DRY-BRINED STEAK

Quality ingredients can stand on their own, and sometimes getting out of the way is the best way to pay respect to your dish. With this dry-brined steakhouse-quality steak, not much more than a little seasoning and some fat is needed to make you want to delete the number of your favorite steakhouse from your phone.

Serves 1

1 (8-ounce) New York strip steak, 1-inch thick

1 teaspoon kosher salt

2 tablespoons clarified butter

pepper, to taste

1. Two to four hours before cooking, evenly season both sides of the steak with kosher salt. Ideally, put the steak on a small cooling rack over a plate and let it rest in the refrigerator until ready to cook, but simply resting on a plate will do fine as well. Through osmosis, the salt will penetrate the meat, initially pulling out some juices and then sucking them back in.

2. When it is time to cook, remove the steak from the refrigerator and transfer it to a room temperature plate. Allow the steak to sit at room temperature for 30 to 45 minutes as you preheat your grill.

3. The hotter you preheat your griddle grill, the quicker the steak will cook, so I prefer bringing my grill to medium-high heat. Put half the clarified butter on the griddle surface and spread it with a spatula to a pool not much larger than the size of your steak. Blot the steak dry with a paper towel or clean kitchen towel and place it in the pool of clarified butter.

4. Use a bacon press to weigh down the steak for about 1 minute and then remove it and cover the meat.

5. Add the remaining clarified butter to the griddle in a pool, and once it begins to shimmer, flip the steak into the pool of butter. Cover the meat and continue to cook for about 4 minutes more. The only real way to accurately cook the steak to your desired doneness is with a probe thermometer. Shoot for a finished temperature of 135°F for medium rare. I will often pull a steak at 131°F and allow it to rest for a few minutes, covered and undisturbed, which allows the temperature to rise a few more degrees to the 135°F I am searching for.

Side Dishes

OKONOMIYAKI SAVORY CABBAGE PANCAKE

The first time I saw a picture of okonomiyaki, I knew I had to make it on the griddle grill. I understand the name of this Japanese style pancake translates to "grilled as you like it," because you can basically add any ingredients you wish to this fun and savory pancake. The foundation of okonomiyaki is typically a cabbage-filled, pancake-like batter, fortified with an egg or two. It's poured onto a hot griddle directly atop thin strips of pork belly or uncured bacon. The pancake is artfully adorned with a Japanese red sauce, which resembles a version of barbecue sauce, and Japanese mayonnaise, which is a bit thicker and a touch sweeter than other mayonnaises. This recipe is designed to be quick to prepare, easy to make, and most of all, fun to eat. If you enjoy making this version, I encourage you to experiment with more traditional Japanese toppings like pickled ginger, bonito flakes, Japanese flour, shrimp, and Chinese sausage. These cakes can be sliced like a pizza and shared, or enjoyed whole—as you like it.

Serves 2 to 4

2 cups shredded cabbage

¼ cup plus 1 tablespoon minced green onion, divided

2 cups Buttermilk Pancake batter (page 23)

4 strips thinly sliced bacon or pork belly

½ cup barbecue sauce

¼ cup hoisin sauce

½ cup mayonnaise

1 teaspoon mirin

black sesame seeds, for garnish

1. In a large bowl, add the shredded cabbage and green onions to the pancake batter and stir to combine.

2. Bring the griddle grill to medium heat. Cut the bacon or pork belly in half slices so you have 8 shorter pieces. Slowly cook the bacon in 2 batches of 4 strips each, in separate areas of the griddle. Adjust the heat if necessary to make sure it is cooking, but not browning and getting crispy just yet, 3 to 5 minutes. A nice pool of rendered bacon fat should be visible.

3. Flip each pile of bacon into the rendered fat and arrange the strips very close together, touching but not overlapping. Using a 1 cup measure, pour the pancake and cabbage mixture onto one of the groups of bacon. The remaining batter goes on the other.

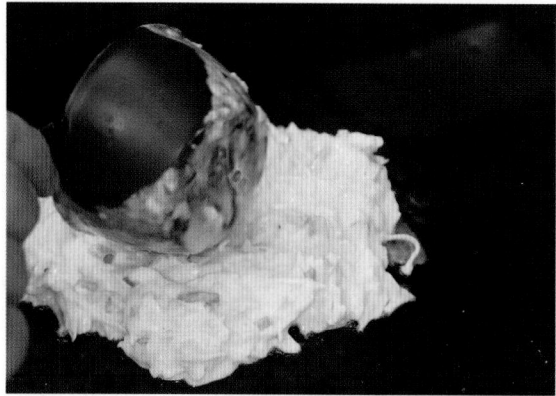

4. Slowly cook the pancake undisturbed for about 5 minutes or until bubbles form and burst, leaving small craters where the bubbles were.

5. Run a long, sturdy spatula under the pancake, taking care to release the bacon from the griddle. When the pancake feels released and slides easily, give it a flip and do the same with the other one. Cook for 3 minutes more.

6. In a small bowl, mix the barbecue sauce with the hoisin. In a separate bowl, mix the mayonnaise with the mirin.

7. Remove the pancakes from the griddle and while they are hot, brush on a thin layer of the hoisin barbecue sauce.

8. Put the mayonnaise mixture in a squeeze bottle and adorn the top of the cabbage cakes with thin ropes of mayonnaise. Garnish with the remaining green onion and sprinkle with black sesame seeds.

FRIED RICE

The base of this fried rice dish is day-old or leftover rice (at least 24 hours old is best). The griddle grill works wonders to reheat and repurpose all kinds of leftover meats and veggies, and a fried rice dish can be as creative as your imagination allows. Although I do prefer using frozen mixed vegetables for fried rice because they cook quicker, the fresh ones will almost always taste better if you cut them into small, evenly diced pieces, and allow crisper items like carrots to sauté a bit longer before adding them to the rice.

Serves 4

½ cup soy sauce

½ cup water

½ cup oyster sauce

2 tablespoons sesame oil

1 tablespoon sriracha (optional)

½ cup finely diced carrots

½ cup diced sweet onions

4 cloves garlic, minced

½ cup frozen peas

4 cups cooked rice, cooled

½ cup finely sliced scallions, divided

cooking oil, as needed

1. In a medium bowl, whisk together soy sauce, water, oyster sauce, sesame oil, and sriracha, if using, and set aside.

2. Bring the griddle grill to medium-high heat and add some cooking oil to the surface. When the oil begins to shimmer, add the carrots, onions, and garlic. Cook, stirring frequently, for about 5 minutes, until the onions begin to turn translucent. Add the peas to the mixture and move to one side of the griddle grill.

3. Add cooking oil to the open space on the griddle and spread the rice out evenly in a single layer. Heat and cook the rice for 3 to 4 minutes, or until it begins to brown a bit.

4. Bring the rice together into a large, tall pile and add about half of the fried rice sauce, half of the scallions, and the cooked vegetables. Using a large spatula, mix the rice and veggies well, then spread the rice back to a single layer on the griddle, allowing the liquids to evaporate and be absorbed in the rice. As the rice absorbs the liquid from the sauce, it will darken. Continue to add fried rice sauce, flipping and mixing the rice until the liquid coats the rice.

5. Transfer the rice onto a serving platter and garnish with the remaining scallions.

BACON JALAPENO– WRAPPED CORN

This dish makes a perfect accompanying act to almost any recipe, but it could star as a lunch all by itself. The sweetness of the corn works great with the saltiness of the bacon, and the punch of heat from the jalapenos is tempered by the cream cheese. I have been cutting corn off of the cob since an orthodontist recommended I do so, but however you enjoy it, I am sure you will find it as ear-resistible as I do.

Serves 2

2 ears corn, shucked

½ cup cream cheese, softened

1 tablespoon smoked paprika

½ cup finely diced seeded jalapeno

6 strips thin-cut bacon

1. Smear the corn with cream cheese. This allows the jalapenos to adhere better. Dust each of the ears of corn with paprika directly onto the cream cheese.

2. Sprinkle the diced jalapenos on a cutting board or flat surface, and then roll the corn through the jalapenos, picking up as many bits of pepper as you can.

3. Start with a strip of bacon at the stalk end and wrap it around the corn. If you give the bacon a bit of a stretch, it often makes a smoother layer and adheres more tightly. Overlap the strips of bacon and wrap until the entire ear of corn is covered. Take care to wrap the bacon tightly so the cream cheese is less likely to leak out.

4. Preheat the griddle to a target temperature of about 300°F.

5. Place bacon-wrapped corn directly on the griddle and cover. Rotate the corn a quarter turn every 2 to 3 minutes. The goal is to both render the bacon and allow the corn to completely cook through.

5. The corn should be done in 15 to 18 minutes, but the slower you render the bacon, the more flavorful the corn becomes.

HOME FRIES WITH VEGGIES

I adore home-fried potatoes. My love for them stems from being able to use leftover ingredients from a previous meal to pull the dish together as a hearty side for breakfast, but it works well for any meal of the day. Using previously baked russet potatoes cuts your cooking time down significantly, and chances are the veggies will be enjoyed by even pickiest palates. Although I love using leftover ingredients for this dish, you can start with fresh, raw potatoes, and veggies. If you are using raw potatoes instead of previously baked, they will take 25 to 35 minutes to fully soften and brown, so plan accordingly.

Serves 4

3 baked russet potatoes, cut to 1-inch cubes

½ cup cooked or frozen broccoli florets

½ cup cooked or frozen diced onion

3 cloves garlic, minced

1 tablespoon garlic salt

1 tablespoon smoked paprika

1 teaspoon pepper

½ cup corn (optional)

½ cup cooked black beans (optional)

½ cup diced ham (optional)

½ cup crumbled cooked sausage (optional)

½ cup diced bacon (optional)

cooking oil, as needed

1. Bring the griddle grill to medium-high heat. Place a good amount of cooking oil on the griddle and when it begins to shimmer, add the diced potatoes in a single layer. Potato pieces will either have three or four sides depending on how they are cut, and you want to allow each of the flat sides to cook for 3 to 5 minutes, adding more oil as needed.

2. While the potatoes are cooking, sauté the broccoli, onion, and garlic for 4 to 5 minutes until lightly browned, stirring or flipping occasionally.

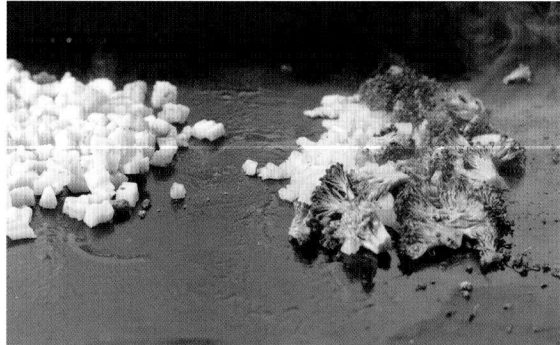

3. When the potatoes are crisp on the outside and creamy in the middle, 10 to 12 minutes, add the vegetable mixture to the potatoes along with the garlic salt, smoked paprika, and pepper. Cook for another 2 to 3 minutes, incorporating any optional ingredients as desired. Serve hot.

RADISH BROWNS WITH BLACK BEANS AND RED PEPPERS

Radishes make a fun alternative to traditional potato hash browns. They are often one of the first root vegetables available for harvest in the late spring. They are a blank flavor canvas and work well with other ingredients, and I love how the black beans and red peppers add both sweet and savory components to this simple dish. I like using coconut oil here because it adds a sweet, nutty flavor, but use whatever oil is your favorite.

Serves 3 or 4

1 bunch radishes, cleaned and grated

½ cup diced red bell pepper

2 cloves garlic, minced

½ cup cooked black beans, drained

1 teaspoon garlic powder

1 teaspoon onion powder

sour cream, to serve

coconut oil or other cooking oil, as needed

salt and pepper, to taste

1. While your griddle grill preheats to medium, cut the tops and bottoms off the radishes. Rinse and clean them well in cold water. The quickest and easiest way to grate the radishes is with a food processor, but if you do not have one available you can use a handheld grater and get the same result.

2. Coat the griddle with a good amount of oil. When the oil begins to shimmer, add the diced red pepper and minced garlic, and cook for about 2 minutes to soften.

3. Add the shredded radishes, black beans, garlic powder, and onion powder to the vegetables, season with salt and pepper, and form a cake about ½ inch thick. Cover and allow the radishes to cook for 4 to 5 minutes, until they begin to brown.

4. Add a bit more cooking oil to the griddle and flip the cake into the new oil once it is hot. Cook for another 3 to 4 minutes, until browned. Serve with a dollop of sour cream, if desired.

NAAN-STYLE FLATBREAD

Naan, pita, and flatbread are all quite similar. Basic ingredients, which are often regionally common or available, are combined to make a simple dough that is cooked on a heated surface instead of baked inside of an oven. These types of breads work great to accompany a meal, but are fantastic for wrapping and holding meats and veggies, or scooping savory dips like hummus.

Serves 8

1 cup warm water

1 teaspoon sugar

1 tablespoon instant dry yeast

3 cups all-purpose flour

½ cup plain yogurt

1 tablespoon olive oil

1 teaspoon salt

cooking oil, as needed

1. In a large bowl, stir together the warm water, sugar, and yeast. Allow the yeast to activate for about 10 minutes.

2. Add all the remaining ingredients, except the cooking oil. Stir until smooth and well combined.

3. Allow the dough to rest, covered, and rise for 1 hour. Turn the dough out onto a floured surface.

4. Bring the griddle grill to medium heat. Divide the dough into eight balls. Roll out each ball into a round about ¼ to ⅛ inch thick.

5. Add a thin coat of oil to the griddle grill and cook the dough rounds for 1 to 2 minutes per side.

GRIDDLE-FRIED RAVIOLI

Normally, ravioli are boiled and quite soft when served. The griddle allows the ravioli to get a crispy and golden exterior, which has a wonderful mouthfeel. Breading the ravioli adds additional flavor and accentuates the crunch.

Serves 4

12 frozen cheese ravioli

½ cup all-purpose flour

1 egg beaten with 2 tablespoons water

1 cup Italian-flavored bread crumbs

¼ cup freshly grated Parmesan cheese

1 tablespoon minced fresh parsley

cooking oil, as needed

marinara sauce, for dipping

1. Spread the frozen ravioli out on a plate and allow them to sit at room temperature for 15 minutes while you bring the griddle grill to medium heat.

2. Place the flour, egg mixture, and bread crumbs in three separate dishes. Dredge the ravioli in flour, then into the egg wash, and then the Italian bread crumbs to develop an even crust. Combine the Parmesan cheese and parsley in a small bowl and set aside.

3. Coat the griddle grill with cooking oil, and when the oil begins to shimmer, place the ravioli in the oil. Allow them to cook without disturbing for about 90 seconds, which will firm up the crust on one side.

4. Flip the ravioli, taking care not to knock off the breading. When the breading has set, you may need to add more oil to the griddle to promote even browning. Cook for 3 to 4 minutes per side, or until the crust gets firm and is golden brown.

5. Remove the ravioli from the griddle and sprinkle with the parsley-cheese mixture while they are still hot enough to melt the cheese. Serve with marinara sauce for dipping.

GRIDDLE-GRILLED VEGGIE EGG ROLLS

Egg rolls are another fun finger food that I love to make because you can put just about anything inside them and they come out amazing. This recipe is simple, but packed with flavor, and a few servings of vegetables too.

Serves 8

8 egg roll wrappers

4 cups bagged coleslaw mix (shredded cabbage and carrots)

2 tablespoons ginger paste

2 tablespoons soy sauce

2 tablespoons sesame oil

1 tablespoon garlic powder

1 teaspoon ground ginger

cooking oil, as needed

1. Keep the egg roll wrappers sealed until just before you construct the egg rolls. Mix all the other ingredients, except the cooking oil, in a large bowl, taking care to coat the veggies with all the spices.

2. Bring the griddle grill to medium heat. Cook the vegetable mixture to wilt the cabbage, soften the carrots, and release moisture from the mixture, 6 to 8 minutes. Cooking the vegetable mixture should diminish it in size by about a third. Set aside on a few paper towels to soak up any additional moisture and allow to cool to at least room temperature.

3. Egg roll wrappers are basically raw pasta sheets. They are susceptible to drying out and acting strange if exposed to air for too long, so when you work with one, keep the others covered and away from liquids. To make an egg roll, place the wrapper on a dry work surface. Spoon about ¼ cup of the vegetable mix onto the bottom third of the wrapper, leaving a border about the width of your pointer finger from the edges. Fill a small bowl with water you can dip your fingers in and finger-paint a small amount of water around the edge of the wrapper, no wider than the width of your finger. Moistening the edges of the wrapper will allow it to adhere to itself. Fold the moistened right and left sides of the wrapper toward the veggies and pinch in place. Take the wrapper side closest to you, and roll the wrapper over the veggies snugly toward the top of the wrapper. The filling should stay inside the wrapper, and the sides should be sealed. Place the egg roll seam-side down on a dry tray and repeat with the remaining ingredients.

4. Bring the griddle grill to medium-high heat. Add cooking oil, and when it begins to shimmer, place the egg rolls on the griddle with the seam sides down. Allow the egg rolls to cook without touching them for 3 to 4 minutes. This will seal the egg rolls shut. Carefully roll the egg rolls on the cooking surface to brown the other sides of the wrappers, adding more cooking oil if necessary. Since the veggies are already cooked, you are just browning the wrapper and heating the veggies back up to temperature.

Snacks, Desserts, and Sauces

POPCORN

This is possibly the perfect snack. You don't need movie night to enjoy popcorn anytime the mood strikes you.

Serves 2 to 4

3 tablespoons peanut oil

½ cup popcorn kernels

3 tablespoons butter

salt, to taste

1. Prepare your griddle for two-zone cooking.

2. Bring the griddle grill to medium-high heat and add the peanut oil. While it is heating, place 5 popcorn kernels in the oil. When 2 or 3 pop, add the butter to the oil and pour in the remaining kernels. Cover immediately with a tall pan or spaghetti pot.

3. When the popcorn starts popping, you will need to stir it in the oil to get all the kernels to pop and prevent the popped corn from burning. Using insulated gloves, potholders, or thick kitchen towels, agitate the popcorn by moving the pan or pot from side to side on the griddle without lifting. Cook for about 4 minutes, or until the popping slows down to once every few seconds.

4. When all the corn is popped, slide the pot or pan and popcorn to the cool side of the grill and remove the lid. Use two spatulas to scoop up the hot popcorn and transfer to a bowl. Serve with salt and additional seasonings as desired.

CHICKPEA CRUNCHERS

This unique recipe is fun to make ahead and pack along on a picnic or keep in the car for your next road trip. The chickpeas (also called garbanzo beans) are a surprisingly satisfying crunchy snack, like a cross between popcorn and a potato chip.

Serves 2

1 (16-ounce) can chickpeas, drained

¼ cup olive oil

1 tablespoon ground cumin

1 tablespoon smoked paprika

1 teaspoon garlic powder

1 teaspoon onion powder

1 teaspoon kosher salt, plus more to taste

1. Combine all ingredients in a large bowl.

2. Pour the mixture onto a cool griddle grill and bring the griddle to medium heat.

3. Allow the mixture to slowly come to temperature and continue to cook, stirring frequently, for up to 30 minutes or until the garbanzo beans have lost most of their moisture and become crispy and crunchy. Finish with additional salt, if desired.

AVOCADO PIZZA BITES WITH BACON-CORN SALSA

A fun play on avocado toast, these bites are a balance of sweet, salty, and creamy flavors with crispy and chewy nuances from the pizza dough. I enjoy how fresh the griddle pizza dough tastes. Here we use pizza dough from a can because it is easy to pack along for tailgating, but you can use your favorite dough from the grocery store or a local pizzeria. So many fun toppings can be added to these avocado bites. I love cooking wafer-thin slices of jalapenos and adding them, as well as cilantro, bell pepper, kalamata olives, and feta or cotija cheese.

Makes about 12, serves 4 to 6

2 small avocados

1 tablespoon lime juice

½ teaspoon garlic salt

½ teaspoon onion powder

dash of hot sauce

1 (13.8-ounce) can pizza dough

4 strips bacon, diced

3 tablespoons olive oil

½ cup corn kernels

1. Remove the pits and stems from the avocados and scrape the flesh from the skins with a spoon. Mash the avocado in a medium bowl with the lime juice, garlic salt, onion powder, and hot sauce. You can make this up to a day ahead, but when the avocado is exposed to air it will quickly discolor, so refrigerate with plastic wrap directly on the avocado to prevent it from discoloring.

2. Bring the griddle grill to medium-high heat. Roll out the pizza dough and cut into about 12 squares, or use a round cookie cutter to cut into 12 disks.

3. On one side of the grill, begin cooking the diced bacon. On the other side, pour about 3 tablespoons of olive oil, and spread it into a very thin layer with a spatula or paper towel. Place the pizza dough on the griddle in the oil and cook the dough for about 90 seconds. Flip, and while the second side of the pizza is cooking, add the corn to the bacon and allow it to cook in the bacon grease.

4. Flip the pizza dough frequently, about every 60 seconds, until it turns golden brown and the dough has cooked through, for a total of 6 minutes.

5. When the bacon is crisp but not burned, about 6 minutes, the corn should also have some color from being cooked on the griddle grill. Scoop the bacon and corn salsa onto a paper towel, allowing the bacon fat to absorb.

6. To assemble, schmear about a tablespoon of the avocado mixture onto the grilled pizza dough and top with a teaspoon of the corn and bacon salsa.

SIMPLE STRAWBERRY SHORTCAKE

I grew up in a town known for having a strawberry farm, and this dessert recipe reminds me of summer there. Although strawberries are now available virtually year-round at national grocery stores, there is something wonderful about getting a pint fresh from the farm and enjoying them immediately.

Serves 6 to 8

4 cups strawberries (about 32)

⅓ cup sugar

1 (16-ounce) can flaky biscuit dough

whipped cream, for garnish

blueberries, for garnish

butter, as needed

1. Hull and quarter the strawberries, and place them in a large bowl. Sprinkle on the sugar and stir to combine. Allow the strawberries to macerate in the sugar and release their juices, for 30 minutes, or up to 2 hours. If you wait longer than that, the berries become mushy.

2. Bring the griddle grill to medium heat and coat the surface with butter. Pop open the can of biscuits and separate them. Sometimes they come out smooshed on one side or looking asymmetrical. If this happens, flatten the biscuit slightly so it has as much surface contact with the griddle as possible.

3. Cook the biscuits in the butter for 4 to 6 minutes per side, or until golden brown and a bit risen.

4. Split the cooked biscuits in half and scoop some of the strawberries and their juices over the cut side. Top with whipped cream and blueberries, if using, add the top half of the biscuit, and enjoy.

GRILLED PINEAPPLE WITH MAPLE WALNUT ICE CREAM

When you grill fruit on the griddle, the natural sugars seem to intensify, tasting sweeter and brighter than when you eat it raw. Pineapple is one of my favorite fruits to grill. Because it is naturally sweet, when it's grilled, it picks up nuances of caramel and some nutty flavors. I prefer using butter, clarified butter, or coconut oil on the griddle grill to cook the pineapple, but any neutral-flavored oil will work.

Serves about 8

1 pineapple, cored and cut into rings, or 1 (16-ounce) can pineapple rings

¼ cup maple syrup

juice of 1 lime

¼ teaspoon ground cinnamon

butter, clarified butter, or coconut oil

1 pint maple walnut ice cream, to serve

chocolate sauce, to serve

1. Bring the griddle grill to medium heat. In a small bowl, stir together the maple syrup, lime juice, and cinnamon, and set aside.

2. Wipe a thin coat of butter or oil on the griddle grill. Place the pineapple in the oil and cook for 3 to 4 minutes, flipping frequently. Use your nose. If you start to smell something burning, it probably is, and you will need to move the pineapple to a cooler part of the griddle.

3. When the pineapple develops some golden color, brush the maple-lime syrup on both sides of the rings. Cook for another 45 seconds per side and remove.

4. Serve with a small scoop of maple walnut ice cream and a drizzle of chocolate sauce.

FOIL-PACKET S'MORES

If you ever had s'mores over a campfire as a kid, you know they are just as enjoyable as an adult. In this recipe, we package the s'mores in foil packets so they can be easily made ahead of time and finished on the griddle grill when you're ready for a sweet treat. It's a perfect project for any dinner guest who is ready to help, but isn't much of a sous chef.

Makes 2

4 graham crackers

1 (1.5-ounce) milk chocolate bar

4 regular-size marshmallows

1. Bring the griddle grill to medium-high heat.

2. Lay down a double layer of heavy-duty aluminum foil in about a 12-inch square on a work surface. Place a graham cracker in the middle of the foil and top it with one-half of the chocolate, then two marshmallows, and another graham cracker on top. Wrap the cracker bundle up in the foil to form a neat pouch with all seams on the top. Repeat with the remaining ingredients to make two pouches total.

3. Place the pouches close together on the griddle grill. Use a squirt bottle to add water to the cook surface to create steam, and immediately cover. Do this again after the s'mores cook for about 2 minutes.

4. Cook the s'mores for 5 to 6 minutes, or until the marshmallows melt. Serve immediately with plenty of napkins.

GRIDDLE SAUCES

Using sauces on the griddle grill can elevate flavors and add additional steam and hydration, which helps the cooking process for many dishes. If you try the sauces on their own, they may taste a little bland. But as they reduce, the flavor intensifies.

I keep griddle sauces in squirt bottles so I can add the right amount of liquid where I need it when I'm cooking. Squirt bottles are much more convenient than using a bowl and a spoon or ladle. When using griddle sauces, squirt enough on the griddle to moisten and surround your food, knowing that the majority of it will evaporate.

I encourage you to try different blends of spices and flavors to enhance the sauces to your liking, but be careful if you're using sugar or juices with a high sugar content, like orange juice, because the sugars can burn at higher temperatures.

ASIAN GRIDDLE SAUCE

Soy sauce and fresh grated ginger bring distinctive Asian flavors to any dish, including the Veggie Stir-Fry (page 77), Ramen Pork and Veggie Cake (page 81), and Asian-Seared Salmon (page 87).

Makes about 2 cups

¾ cup water

½ cup mirin

½ cup soy sauce

¼ cup sesame oil

1 tablespoon garlic powder

1 tablespoon ground ginger

1 tablespoon grated fresh ginger

Put ingredients in a medium bowl and whisk until combined. Use immediately or store refrigerated for up to 10 days.

BALSAMIC GRIDDLE SAUCE

This versatile sauce works especially well with meats, as in the Steak and Mushroom with Balsamic Sauce crepe on page 39.

Makes about 2 cups

1¼ cups balsamic vinegar

½ cup water

¼ cup honey

¼ cup cooking oil

1 tablespoon Italian seasoning

1 teaspoon salt

1 teaspoon white pepper

Put ingredients in a medium bowl and whisk until combined. Use immediately or store refrigerated for up to 10 days.

LEMON GRIDDLE SAUCE

Brighten up dishes, like the Chicken Fajita Sandwich on page 57, with the zing of lemon.

Makes about 2 cups

1 cup low-sodium chicken broth

½ cup freshly squeezed lemon juice

¼ cup cooking oil

¼ cup water

1 tablespoon finely minced fresh chives

1 tablespoon fresh thyme

1 tablespoon finely minced garlic

Put ingredients in a medium bowl and whisk until combined. Use immediately or store refrigerated for up to 10 days.

WHITE WINE GRIDDLE SAUCE

A mix of white wine and sherry adds a lovely sweetness to recipes, like the Scallops and Asparagus Tips on page 89.

Makes about 2 cups

1 cup dry white wine

½ cup water

¼ cup cooking sherry

¼ cup cooking oil

2 tablespoons finely minced shallots

1 tablespoon dried parsley

1 tablespoon finely minced garlic

1 tablespoon finely minced capers

1 teaspoon salt

1 teaspoon pepper

Put ingredients in a medium bowl and whisk until combined. Use immediately or store refrigerated for up to 10 days.

SPICY BBQ GRIDDLE SAUCE

The Spicy BBQ griddle sauce complements a variety of meats and vegetables on the griddle. I especially like using it with the Behemoth Bacon Burgers (page 51) for a sweet and spicy component to the sandwich.

Makes about 2 cups

1 cup ketchup

⅓ cup cider vinegar

⅓ cup apple juice

¼ cup Worcestershire sauce

¼ cup sriracha

2 tablespoons water

2 tablespoons onion powder

2 tablespoons garlic powder

2 tablespoons sugar

2 tablespoons brown sugar

2 tablespoons tomato paste

Put ingredients in a medium bowl and whisk until combined. Use immediately or store refrigerated for up to 10 days.

Conversion Charts

Volume Conversions

U.S.	U.S. Equivalent	Metric
1 tablespoon (3 teaspoons)	½ fluid ounce	15 milliliters
¼ cup	2 fluid ounces	60 milliliters
⅓ cup	3 fluid ounces	90 milliliters
½ cup	4 fluid ounces	120 milliliters
⅔ cup	5 fluid ounces	150 milliliters
¾ cup	6 fluid ounces	180 milliliters
1 cup	8 fluid ounces	240 milliliters
2 cups	16 fluid ounces	480 milliliters

Weight Conversions

U.S.	Metric
½ ounce	15 grams
1 ounce	30 grams
2 ounces	60 grams
¼ pound	115 grams
⅓ pound	150 grams
½ pound	225 grams
¾ pound	350 grams
1 pound	450 grams

Temperature Conversions

Fahrenheit (°F)	Celsius (°C)	Fahrenheit (°F)	Celsius (°C)
70°F	20°C	220°F	105°C
100°F	40°C	240°F	115°C
120°F	50°C	260°F	125°C
130°F	55°C	280°F	140°C
140°F	60°C	300°F	150°C
150°F	65°C	325°F	165°C
160°F	70°C	350°F	175°C
170°F	75°C	375°F	190°C
180°F	80°C	400°F	200°C
190°F	90°C	425°F	220°C
200°F	95°C	450°F	230°C

Acknowledgments

I would like to thank Victoria Townsend of Dash of Savory for her help styling and photographing many of the dishes. She took shots both on and off the grill for:

Bacon on the grill (page 9)

Buttermilk Pancakes (page 23)

Pigs in a Blanket (page 31)

Eggs Belledict (page 32)

Diner-Style Omelet (page 35)

Strawberry, Banana, and Hazelnut-Chocolate Crepes (page 41)

Chicken Bacon Artichoke Crepes (page 42)

Behemoth Bacon Burgers (page 51)

#ChoppedCheese (page 52)

Chicken Fajita Sandwich on a Quesadilla Bun (page 57)

Ground Pork Banh Mi (page 63)

Cuban Sandwich (page 65)

Shrimp with Cheesy Polenta Cakes (page 78)

Ramen Pork and Veggie Cake (page 81)

Asian-Seared Salmon (page 87)

Scallops and Asparagus Tips (page 89)

Okonomiyaki Savory Cabbage Pancake (page 95)

Popcorn (page 111)

Chickpea Crunchers (page 113)

Avocado Pizza Bites with Bacon-Corn Salsa (page 114)

Grilled Pineapple with Maple Walnut Ice Cream (page 119)

Victoria has an amazing eye for detail and brings a plating style I would not have been able to have achieved without her help. I encourage you to follow along with what she is cooking at her website https://dashofsavory.com or on Instagram @dashofsavory.

About the Author

Grill master **Paul Sidoriak** created the website GrillingMontana.com to showcase his culinary successes and failures on the grill. Paul uses his grills as a blank canvas and a creative place to make delicious foods. This book is a nostalgic look at some of the dishes he cooked three decades ago, which have evolved as his cooking style has matured. His dishes are lighthearted, whimsical, and seasonally based, taking advantage of what is in season whenever possible. Paul grills year-round at his home in western Montana, regardless of whether Mother Nature decides to cooperate. Follow what Paul has cooking and say hello on Instagram @GrillingMontana, Twitter @GrillingMontana, or on Facebook at www.facebook.com/GrillingMontana.